Aldborough

The Village in the Suburbs

A History

Ron Jeffries

May 2017

Published by the author

First published in Great Britain in 2012
First printing March 2012
Second printing May 2012
Third printing – Revised and updated – April 2017

*Some sections of the text were first published in the
BROADSHEET, the monthly newsletter of
St. Peter's Aldborough Hatch, Essex*

Copyright © Ron Jeffries 2012

The right of Ron Jeffries to be identified as the Author of the Work has been asserted by him in accordance with the
Copyright, Designs and Patents Act 1988.
All rights reserved. No part of this publication may be reproduced, stored in a retrieval system, or transmitted, in any form or by any means without the prior written permission of the publisher, nor be otherwise circulated in any form of binding or cover other than that in which it is published and without a similar condition being imposed on the subsequent purchaser.

A CIP catalogue record for this title is available from the British Library.

Paperback ISBN 978-0-9561877-2-7

Printed and bound in England by SPS Print

Published at
37 Spearpoint Gardens
Aldborough Road North
Aldborough Hatch
ILFORD
Essex IG2 7SX
United Kingdom

Email: ronjeffries@live.co.uk

By the same author
Programme Planning in the Scout Troop
The Outdoor Adventure Book for Cub Scouts and all boys
The Whizz Kids Book of Camping (with Paul Moynihan)
The Scout Troop – A handbook for Scout Leaders and Patrol Leaders
(with Paul Moynihan)
Just an Essex Lad – An autobiography
Long forgotten, now remembered – a sequel to Just an Essex Lad

Dedication

I dedicate this revised and updated Edition to my ever-loving wife for 57 years and my companion at my side today,
Yvonne,
whose patience knew no bounds in her lifetime and who must now be surprised to discover that I am able to cook, cope with the washing, manage some ironing, do the shopping and online banking, keep the garden tidy, liaise with the neighbours and change the beds (the latter under supervision, of course), whilst having the support of my wonderful family and many friends. Yvonne loved Aldborough Hatch, in general, and St. Peter's Church, in particular (where she was a life-long member of the choir and Sacristan for nearly 30 years), and would be distraught to learn that this unofficial history was out of print.
Hence this 2017 edition.

Note on third printing

This book has been out of print for three years or so. During that time I have received requests for copies which I have been unable to fulfil – hence this third printing. I have taken the opportunity to update some of the factual information and to substitute one photograph. Four new pages numbered 115 to 118 have been added with fresh text and four photographs.

Acknowledgements

I am grateful to so many good friends who have helped me with my research – I trust I have not been too demanding in my endeavours.

My thanks to the following (and my apologies to those whose names I have inadvertently omitted): John and Jenifer Allen, Graham and Pat Borrott, Linda Bowley, Elsie Briscoe, Lucie Burrow, Ruth Chomyn, Ruth Clarke, Vanessa Cole, Peter Collins, John Coombes, David Davis, John Debere, Brian Ecott, Revd. Jonathan Evens, Diane Foster, Chris, Margaret and Sheryl Gannaway, Bob and Mary Garrett, Geoffrey Gillan, Ray Haw, Carole Holme, Doreen Howard, Judith Jacobs, Gaby Laws, David Martin, Margaret Merritt, Daphne Padfield, Colin Perrin, Mick and Jeanette Pointing, Loraine Porter, John Roper, Shirley Rudge, Balkrishna Savant, Amanda and Peter Schlotter, Derek Smith, Val Smith, Frances and Michael Speakman, Martyn and Pat Stewart, Foster Summerson, Bernard Thomas, Keith Tranmer, John Whitworth, Ann and Clive Wilderspin, Raymond Woolmore, Adrian and Chris Wyatt. And to all my friends in Aldborough Hatch, Barkingside, Ilford and the wider community whose encouragement and enthusiasm has made writing this book a pleasure. Special thanks to my family for their patience when I repeat the same story for the umpteenth time (and, kindly folk that they are, they just smile).

My thanks to Revd Kate Lovesey, Priest-in-Charge, and Brian Kerrison, Reader, both at St. Peter's Church; to former Churchwardens Roger Goffee, Chris Kerrison and Roger Kirby; and members and former members of the Parochial Church Council, including Pam Goffee, Irene Kirby and Linda Wright, for their support and giving me access to the church archives.

I am grateful to the Hainault Forest website for permission to use material; to the Essex Record Office for their helpful advice; to the Revd. Nick Wheeler, LVO, Ecclesiastical Secretary, Crown Ecclesiastical Office, Cabinet Office; to Brian J. Hood of the Diocesan Registry, Diocese of Chelmsford, and Anna Franklin, BA (Hons), Property/Glebe Officer, Diocese of Chelmsford – all of whom set me on the right path; Krzysztof Adamiec, Lambeth Palace Library for permission to use the plan on page 24; to Ian Dowling, Redbridge Local Studies and Archive, and Simon J. Algar, Building Conservation Officer, London Borough of Redbridge.

I acknowledge information culled from British History Online – *The ancient parish of Barking: Roman Catholicism and Protestant Nonconformity* and *The borough of Ilford, A History of the County of Essex: Volume 5 (1966)*; from *Ilford Past and Present* by George Tasker (1901); *A Sketch of Ancient Barking: Its Abbey, And Ilford* (1899) by Edward Tuck; *A potted history of Ilford* (1997) by Norman Gunby; *The London Gazette*; *Alan Godfrey Maps*. Thanks to the internet and Google.

Finally, thanks to Simon Smith of SPS Print for his valued help in bringing this revised version of my book to life, and for his patience and fortitude in dealing with my often unreasonable requests.

Contents

	Page
A dip into the past	1
Aldbro' Hatch – according to Edward Tuck	2
Hainault Forest	3
Aldborough Hatch 1786	5
Aldborough Hatch 1844	6
A railway line through Aldborough Hatch!	7
Aldborough Hatch 1905	9
Aldborough Hatch 1914	10
The Chapel at Aldborough Hatch	11
The Chapel of St. James, Little Heath	16
Westminster Bridge	19
The New Chapel at Aldborough Hatch	20
The London Gazette and the Vicars of Aldborough Hatch	25
Churchwardens of Aldborough Hatch	29
St. Peter's Vicarage	31
St. Peter's Aldborough Hatch over the years	37
Aldborough Church School and Church Halls	44
The Organ at St. Peter's	46
The Sculpture: *And other sheep I have* – Anthony Foster	49
The Painting: *The Crucifixion* – Leonard Wyatt	51
The Sculpture: *The Woman of Samaria* – Thomas Bayliss Huxley-Jones	53
The Stained Glass Windows at St. Peter's	55
The Lychgate at St. Peter's	58
The Artefacts at St. Peter's	59
The Jewish Grave at St. Peter's	62
The Churchyard at St. Peter's	64
St. Peter's Flower Festivals	71
Aldborough Hall and Equestrian Centre	74
The Dick Turpin – From Beer House to Public House to Restaurant	76
Cuckoo Hall	80
St. Chad's Well	81
The Farms and Farmhouses of Aldborough Hatch	82
Aldborough House Farm	83
Aldborough Hatch Farm	86
Aldborough Hall Farm	88
The Smithy	89
Willow Farm	90
Whites Farm	91
Hainault Farm	93
Fairlop Airfield	94
Fairlop Waters Country Park	96
Aldborough Grange and Grange Estate	99
Abury House	101
Newbury Park Station	102
Ilford War Memorial Gardens	104
The Rich and the Famous	106
Some little-known facts	110
Listed Buildings in Aldborough Hatch	114
2017 Updates	115

Introduction

Let's get one thing crystal clear from the start. This is *not* an official history of Aldborough Hatch – nor, for that matter, is it an unofficial history. Rather it is a journey and a somewhat rambling one at that – a bit like my life in some ways. My journey started in 1933 in the Ilford Maternity Hospital (where the Holiday Inn Express Hotel stands today), within a stone's throw of Newbury Park Station (now on London Underground's Central Line) and within walking distance of Aldborough Hatch in the then Borough of Ilford and today the London Borough of Redbridge, but which we continue to declare is in the County of Essex (which it clearly is not, but woe betide anyone who throws doubt on this!). And I lived my life in Newbury Park, briefly in the centre of Ilford, and for yonks in Aldborough Hatch (with many journeys around the UK and even some abroad).

This book has its origins in 1988 when St. Peter's Church in Aldborough Hatch staged its eighth Flower Festival celebrating 125 years of the church (a year late as we recently discovered!). Local historian, the late Frank Sainsbury, gave me much valued assistance in compiling a brief history of Aldborough Hatch and the church, published in the Festival Brochure and later uploaded onto the church website (www.stpetersah.org.uk). In 2007 I wrote, and St. Peter's published, an eight-page booklet *From Westminster to Aldborough Hatch – A History of St. Peter's Church*. My research has taken me far and wide. Much of the information in these pages is factually correct, but some is anecdotal, but I make no apologies, for – as I wrote above – this is not official or even unofficial.

If St. Peter's Church features large in this book this is because it has been at the very heart of Aldborough Hatch for the past 155 years – and, as revealed here with evidence, was consecrated in 1862 and not 1863 as I will show. Deciding what to put in the book and what to leave out has been a problem. Space precludes including every building of historical interest in Aldborough Hatch and I apologise for the omissions. It saddens me – and may well distress you – that I have been unable to cover fully the William Torbitt Primary School, which opened its doors in 1937 and was built as the result of the expanding population in this neck of the woods. I attended the William Torbitt in 1938 and it was here where my children and one grandchild started their education, with one ending up at Lady Margaret Hall, Oxford University. It has two excellent websites to which I would direct you (School: www.williamtorbitt.org.uk; For Former Pupils: www.williamtorbitt.co.uk/history.asp). Nor will you find more than fleeting glances at King George, Chadwell Heath and Goodmayes Hospitals. In the first I had my tonsils removed as a three-year-old when the hospital was based near Newbury Park Station. In the second I was poorly with diphtheria at the age of seven. And in my retirement I walked the corridors of Goodmayes as a non-executive director of the North East London Mental Health NHS Trust. And in view of over 60 years involvement with and commitment to The Scout Association, it is a near tragedy and almost criminal that I have been unable to make any reference to Hargreaves Scout Camp Site and Activity Centre in Hainault Road – but perhaps there will be another book in the years to come . . . Watch this space, as they say!

A dip into the past

I will start with a brief skirmish into the dark days of the past – to set the scene. After the Norman Conquest by William the Conqueror (which began on 28th September 1066), Ilford was part of the Manor of Barking, held by the Abbey of Barking, founded around AD 666 and demolished in 1541-2. As for Aldborough Hatch, according to the *Oxford Dictionary of London Place Names* (2001), the earliest recorded use of the name is Aldborough Hacche (c.1490). I was not around at the time, so I will take the word of the author, Mr A. Mills, for it. After the Dissolution (1536 to 1541) – when Henry VIII got a bit stroppy, disbanding the monasteries to became Supreme Head of the Church of England - the estates were split and one centred on Aldborough Hatch was developed by Bartholomew Barnes (who died in 1548). The estate remained in the family until 1668, when it was divided between two sisters, Abigail and Hester, the former taking the central section based on Aldborough Hatch Farm, the latter an outer section which included Aldborough House Farm but also areas to the east and north. Both estates eventually passed into other hands, with part being sold to the Crown in 1828 and that of Aldborough Hatch Farm being acquired by the Revd. G. Stevens in the early 19th Century and remaining in his family until 1929 when it, too, was sold to the Crown. The Aldborough House Farm estate was acquired, through marriage, by a Colonel Martin Bladen in the 1720s and he was responsible for rebuilding the manor house around 1728 as a large red brick mansion, the approach to which was along what is today the Bridleway 93 running west from St. Peter's Church. Aldborough House – which stood roughly equidistant from, and slightly to the east of, the two farms – was demolished circa 1808.

The view across the fields from St. Peter's Church in 2008 with Lake Cottages (far left) and Aldborough Hatch Farm (centre) with barns (far right). Aldborough House Farm is way over to the left and out of the photograph.

But what of Ilford? It was created as a separate ecclesiastical parish in 1830 with the building of St. Mary's Church in the High Road. In 1888 Ilford took over its own municipal responsibilities, electing its own council. It was a large village with a population in 1891 of 10,913, growing to 42,000 by 1899. In 1926 Ilford became a Municipal Borough and in 1965 it was merged with Wanstead and Woodford to form the London Borough of Redbridge – the jolly place it is today with its own Council and Mayor and all that stuff. But I am racing ahead of myself . . .

Aldbro' Hatch – according to Edward Tuck

Born in 1819, Edward Tuck's father was an architect and builder's surveyor in London. At his father's death, Ilford became his adopted home where the Vicar of Ilford, the Revd. Canon Leighton encouraged him to train as a teacher. Qualifying at the National Societies' Training College, Westminster, he later became Headmaster of the Boys' National School Ilford. In 1899, Edward Tuck wrote a book – *A Sketch of Ancient Barking: Its Abbey, And Ilford* - which includes the following snapshot of the history of Aldborough Hatch as he saw it at the turn of the 19th Century. In a few sentences he encapsulates centuries of history. Some dates and spellings differ from other records we have consulted, and in some cases the same surname is spelt in two different ways in the same paragraph.

Aldbury, Aldborough, or Aldbro' Hatch was a capital mansion, with lands, situate in the forest about four miles from Barking Church. The name denotes an 'old seat near a hatch or low-gate'. This was the property of Bartholomew Baron, or Barnes, who died in 1541; his grandson, Thomas Barnes, died seised of it in 1626. John Lockey, Esq., was the owner of the estate about the beginning of the 17th Century, he died in 1737, when the moiety of the estate was sold to Richard Guise, Esq. There was a good house on the estate. This portion of the estate now belongs to the Breame family. The other moiety came into possession of Colonel Jory, who died in 1725, and left it to his niece, Frances, who married Martin Bladin, Esq., one of the Lords of Trade. Mr Bladin built a mansion on his portion of the estate at an expense of £14,000. His widow left it to her cousin, Ann Hodges, who in 1737 had been married to her second husband, John Lambert Middleton, Esq., brother of Sir William Middleton, Bart. Mrs Bladen, by her will bearing date 1746, endowed the Aldboro' Hatch chapel with £20 per annum for ever, charged upon the estate, and gave the sacramental plate. This estate fell into the hands of the Crown, who, till within a few years dealt out with a niggard hand the afore-named £20 per annum but, owing to the great exertions of the late incumbent, the Revd. J. M. Proctor, and his predecessor, the Revd. J. Godding, a pretty little church has been erected in lieu of the old chapel, and in addition an excellent parsonage house, with schoolrooms, etc. (The latter being references to St. Peter's Church, Vicarage and Aldborough Hatch Church of England School.)

The reference to the *"niggard hand"* of the Crown is a theme taken up by George Tasker in *Ilford Past and Present*, published two years later in 1901, where he refers to the *"folly and short-sightedness of the Crown in 1851"* when over 100,000 trees were cut down in Hainault Forest – but more of that later . . . Meantime, George Tasker records that *"for many centuries before the Tudor period nearly all the land within a wide radius of Barking belonged to the Abbess and Convent of that place . . . Barking Parish was divided into four wards of which Ilford was one"*. In 1830 Ilford was formed into a distinct parish of which Barkingside and Aldborough Hatch were part – in 1841 Barkingside became a separate parish, followed in 1863 by Aldborough Hatch. George describes Fairlop Plain as *"exceedingly flat, dreary and uninteresting"* – I would challenge him on that were he alive today for it is something I intend to disprove in this book.

Hainault Forest

The Chapman and Andre Map of 1777 *(above)* shows the extent of Hainault – spelt Henhault – Forest at that time, stretching down to Abury Gate and Abury Hatch, forerunners of Aldborough Hatch, and running from Barkingside to Collier Row and Padnall Corner. Note Mossfoot (Mossford) Green, Hog Hill Pond, Henhault Lodge and the location of the Fairlop Oak tree (of which more later). But

3

we need to go further back in time to see how the forest changed and the name developed. Following the Perambulation of the Forest of Essex in 1641 in the reign of Charles I, the exact boundaries of the forest were established ('perambulation' indicating that this was accomplished by 'walking around'). The River Lea formed a natural boundary in the west, with the highway from Bow Bridge to Ilford and the Whalebone Road the southern boundary and a series of stones formed the eastern boundary. The forest was bisected by the River Roding from Passingford Bridge north of the Richard Stone to Ilford. It was a natural division – one half became known as Waltham Forest and the other Hainault Forest *(coloured green)*. At the time that Henry VIII got stroppy, the woodland became the King's own property within Hainault Forest which was still subject to Forest Laws. The woodland became known as Kings Wood. As to the derivation of the present name of Hainault Forest, P. H. Reaney in his book *The Place-names of Essex* (1935) and W. R. Fisher in *The Forest of Essex* (1887) list variant spellings as follows:

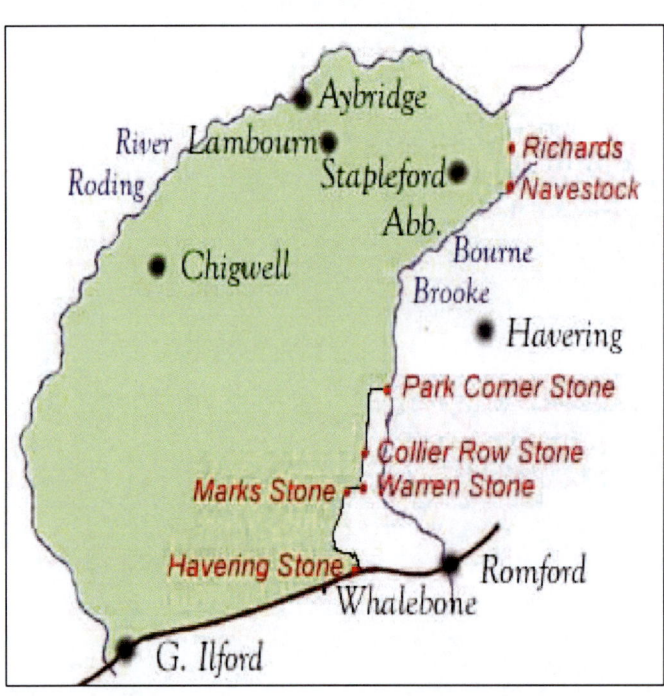

1221 Henehout
1239 Hynehol
1251 Hyneheut
1251 Foresta de Hineheut
1323 Hineho
1323 Hynehalte, Hyneholte

1348 Henholt
1475 Hennold, Chappell Hennold, Hennolde
1513 Heynold, Inholt
1590 Chapple Heinault,
1654 West Hainault, Heyault, Heynault
1777 Henhault – in late Victorian times Hainhault appears on maps and texts

P. H. Reaney concludes that all the above spellings come from the roots *higna* and *holt* – *Higna* being a monastic community and *holt* woodland. "*The modern spelling is due to a fictitious connection with Philippa of Hainault or Hainaut in Belgium, Queen Consort to Edward III*" (born 1314, married 1328, died 1369). So there we have it! How the Belgians became involved is cloaked in mystery. All somewhat confusing, but history is often thus.

Aldborough Hatch 1786

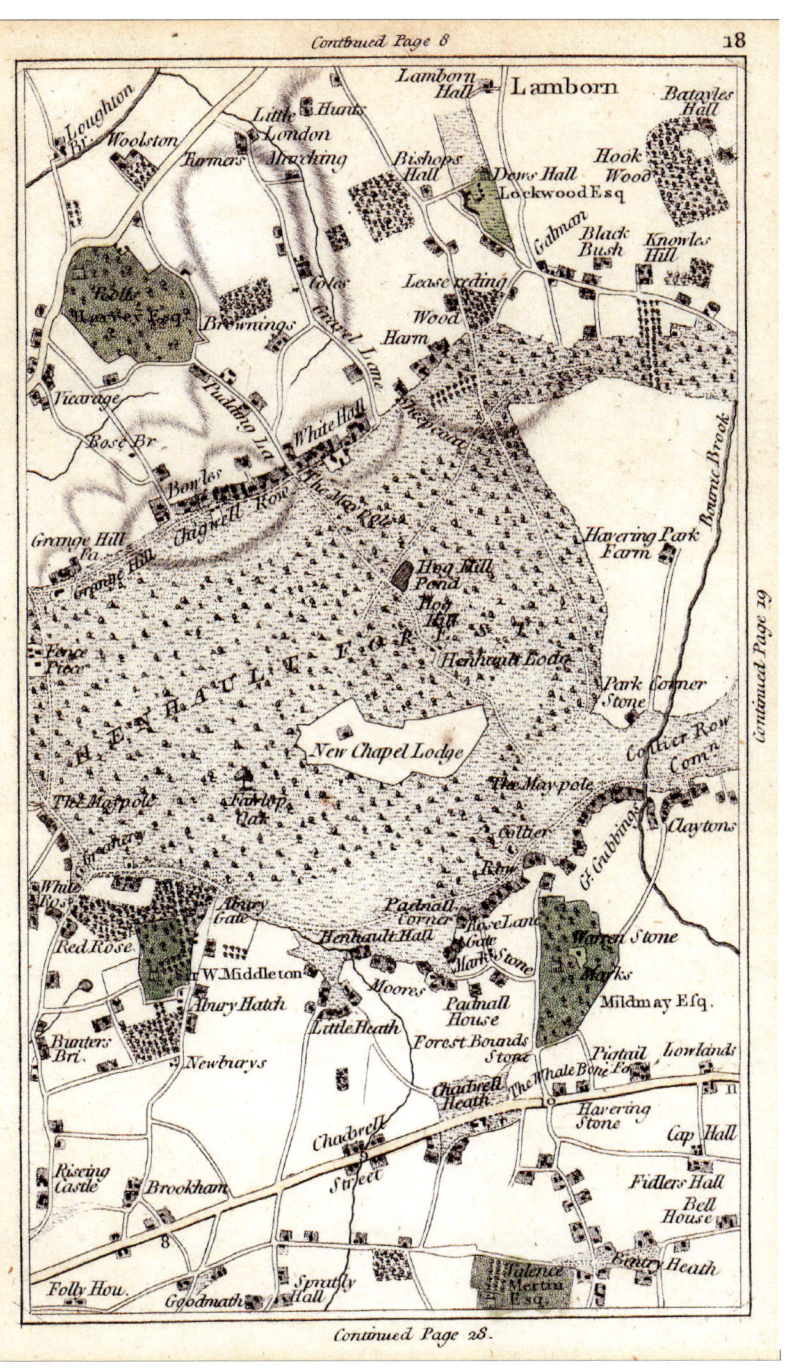

This Map of Henhault Forest, Essex, is taken from Cary's survey of 15 miles around London, dated 1786. Henhault Forest stretched down as far as Abury Hatch – the word 'hatch' referred to a wicket gate into the forest. The Fairlop Oak is marked above Abury Gate as are Hog Hill and Hog Hill Pond. The route of Oaks Lane is marked from Aldborough Road via Chase Lane to Horns Road.

Aldborough Hatch 1844

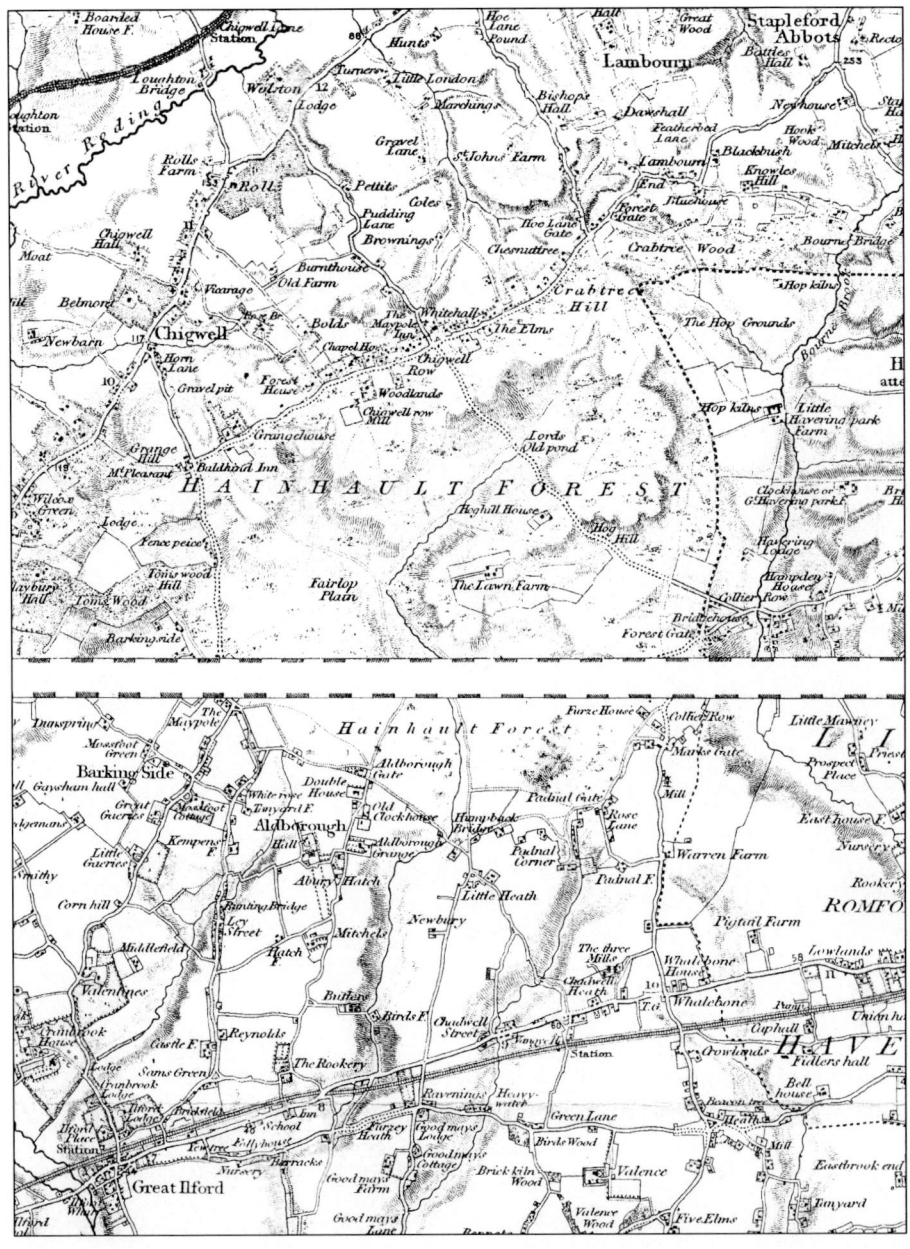

Taken from a reprint of the first edition of the one-inch Ordnance Survey map of England and Wales dated 1844; you will be able to make out Aldborough Gate, the Old Clockhouse, Aldborough Grange, Abury Hatch and Aldborough.

A railway line through Aldborough Hatch!

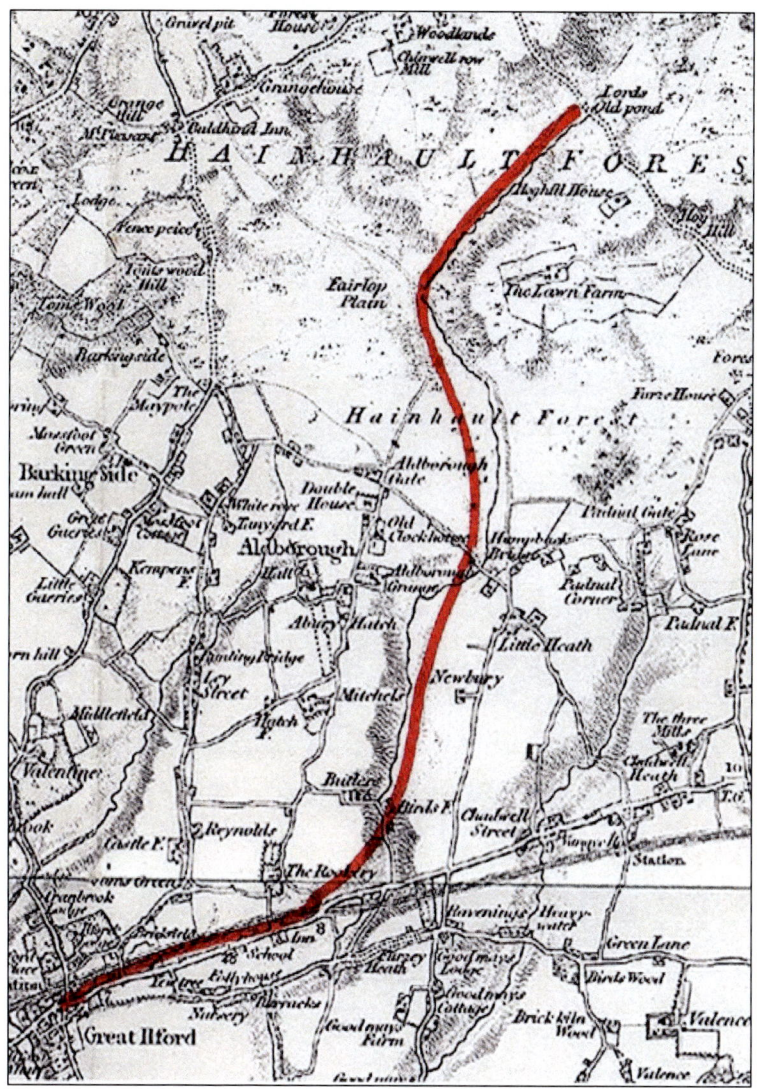

Many of us thought we had a war on our hands in the 1990s when the London City All-Weather Racecourse was proposed for Fairlop Waters, but imagine the furore that would arise today if a railway line was proposed through our beloved Aldborough Hatch, for that's what happened – but it was long ago . . . in 1857!

The Eastern Counties Railway line through Ilford had been in existence for about 20 years when a plan and proposal for a branch line was lodged at Essex County Hall in 1857. Railway lines were springing up all over the Country and were fragmented and owned by small companies. There often appeared to be no regard as to whether a railway would have sufficient passengers and freight to support it. The Hainhault (yes, that's how it was spelt!) Forest Railway was designed by Engineer Richard B. Grantham FGS. The total length of the planned branch line would be five miles and eight-and-a-half chains. The railway line would start at Ilford Station and run eastwards for one mile, then branch northwards following Seven Kings Water to Hainhault Forest, terminating at Lord's Old Pond. In case, like me, you are wondering what a chain was, land surveyors' linear measures prior to metrication were as follows:

1 link = 7.92 inches
1 chain = 100 links
10 chains = 1 furlong

8 furlongs = 1 mile
1 acre = 0.4047 hectares
2.71 acres = 1 hectare (10,000m^2)

So now you know, but then I expect you did in any case! I will admit that I did not, but then there are many things of which I am totally ignorant, but then you knew that already.

The route of the line is shown on the previous page superimposed on the first edition Ordnance Survey map dated 12th July 1844. In 1851 – as I will never tire of advising readers through these pages – Hainault Forest was disafforested and almost immediately 100,000 trees belonging to the Crown were cut down. The cleared area was divided up into Crown farms like Foxburrows, Forest, Aldborough Hall, Aldborough House, Aldborough Hatch and Hainault Farms – amongst others – which were set up in 1856/7. New roads were built – New North Road, Forest Road and Hainault Road: while the Chigwell Row to Collier Row road was improved. The restored Hainault Forest came into being in 1903/6.

What was the purpose of the railway? What did the shareholders aim to achieve? It could have been for residents of Chigwell Row for travel to Ilford and London. It may be that produce (milk, grain, vegetables) from the farms would be transported to the markets in London. But the line was never built and we shall, therefore, never know if a group of concerned residents would have risen up to protest at the potential desecration of Fairlop Plain and its environs and given Essex County Council a run for their money as we have done with recent developers and, to a lesser extent, Redbridge Council. That was when the Aldborough Hatch Defence Association and Barkingside 21, with the backing of a number of friendly Councillors, Greater London Authority Members, Members of Parliament and others mounted fervent opposition to the building of the London City All-weather Racecourse in the early part of this century at Fairlop Waters *(see page 96).*

There are some folk who will tell you that a bus route used to run along Aldborough Road North, terminating at St. Peter's Church, but if there was I missed it. It is a fact, however, that under the *Ilford Urban District Council Tramways Act 1904,* an extension to the tram system in Ilford was proposed from Cameron Road in Seven Kings, up Aldborough Road to St. Peter's – but it never happened and eventually trolley buses replaced the trams in Ilford from 1938.

Aldborough Hatch 1905

From the Ordnance Survey Romford Sheet 257 – 1905 (not to scale). Hainault Forest may be seen in the top right-hand corner of the map – although oddly and somewhat perversely, the words appear over what is known today as Fairlop Plain. Forest Road may be seen running from Hog Hill to Fullwell Hatch in Barkingside. Aldborough Hall (where the Equestrian Centre stands today) and Aldborough Hall Farm are both clearly marked, but (again oddly and perversely) neither Aldborough House Farm nor Aldborough Hatch Farm are so designated by the map-makers

Hainault Forest Country Park is one of the few remaining sections of the former Forest of Essex in England. Epping Forest and Hatfield Forest are other examples.

In a survey for stroppy Henry VIII in 1544 the extent of Hainault Forest was some 3,000 acres; today it is 336 acres.

Aldborough Hatch 1914

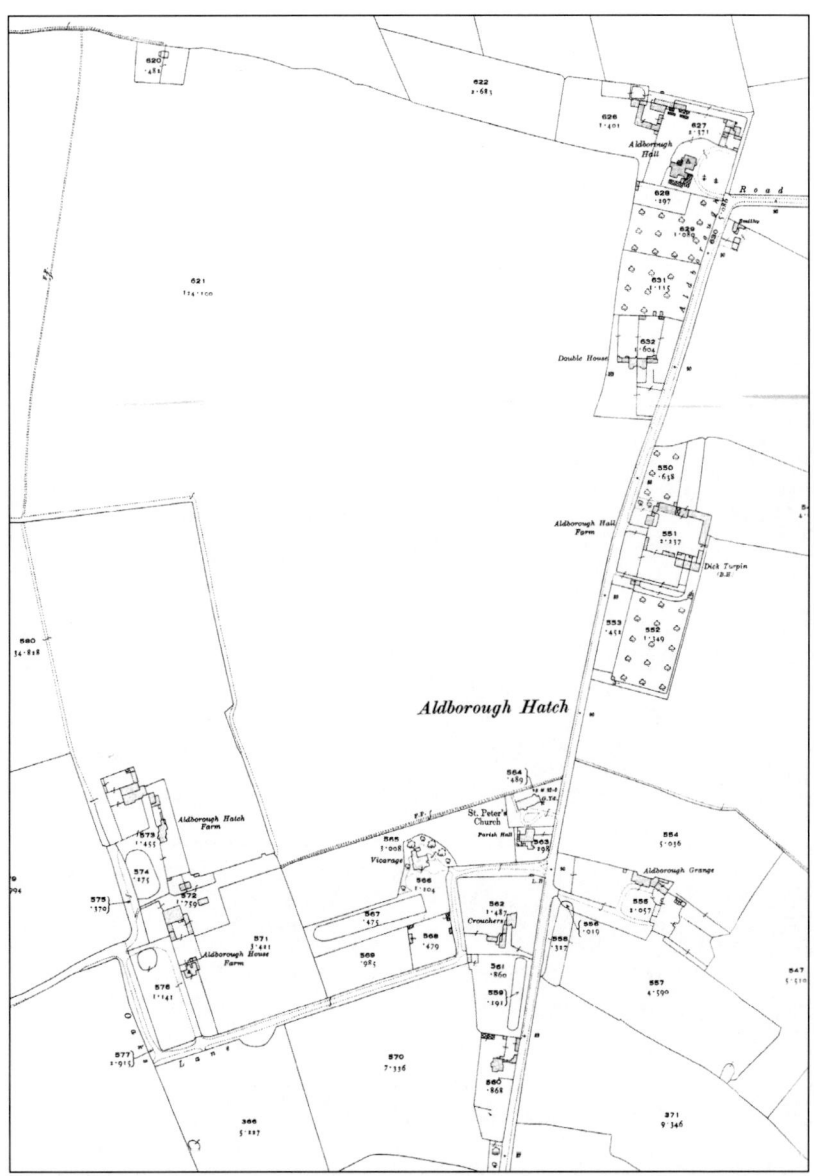

This map (above) is reduced from the Ordnance Survey 15 inches to the mile map dated 1914 (and is not to scale). Aldborough Hall, the Smithy, Double House, Aldborough Hall Farm, the Dick Turpin beer house, St. Peter's (and the extent of the Churchyard at that time), the Vicarage garden, lake and meadow, Aldborough Hatch and House Farms, and Aldborough Grange are all marked.

The Chapel at Aldborough Hatch

We have mentioned earlier that Aldborough Hatch was part of the Manor of Barking. There is evidence of strong Puritanism in Barking in the early 17th century. The following has been culled from *The ancient parish of Barking: Roman Catholicism and Protestant Nonconformity, A History of the County of Essex: Volume 5* (1966), pp. 231-233.

"During the Civil War and Interregnum this showed itself not only by the appointment of lecturers and in schemes for parochial reorganisation, but also in the formation of a Quaker meeting. There is even a hint, in 1655, of Unitarian activities, the suppression of which was ordered by the government. After the Restoration (of the monarchy which began in 1660) *Edward Kighley, minister of the new chapel at Aldborough Hatch, appears to have been ejected from his cure, and in 1672 he was licensed as a Presbyterian to teach and preach in his house at Aldborough Hatch.*

"A Presbyterian congregation, said to number 200, existed at Aldborough Hatch in 1690-2, with John Gidleigh as minister. Another nonconformist minister connected with Aldborough Hatch was Edward Whiston (who died in 1697), who is said to have preached there twice every Sunday even when over 90. There is also a reference to Samuel Hardy, who was 'chaplain to Esquire Heal at Overy Hatch' between 1683 and 1690. Hardy's employer was presumably John Neale (who died in 1698), owner through his wife of one of the moieties into which the Aldborough Hatch estate was divided after the death of Isabel Kighley, mother of the above Edward Kighley.

"It seems probable, therefore, that from the Restoration until the end of the 17th century the Presbyterian congregation gathered at Aldborough Hatch House, under the patronage first of the Kighleys and then of the Neales. There is no evidence that it continued to meet after John Neale's death, when the estate passed to Richard Jory, but it is possible that the chapel at Aldborough Hatch House, which Jory's niece, Frances Bladen, later endowed for Anglican worship, had been used by the Presbyterians in the previous century."

So Aldborough Hatch Chapel on Aldborough House Farm possibly pre-dates Aldborough House to which it was attached and it may have been built in the late 17th or early 18th Century. It is a Grade II Listed Building; the List Entry Description refers to it as the Barn at Aldborough House Farm and reads: *"Circa 1730. Formerly the chapel attached to Aldborough Hall. Small rectangular building with steep pitch tile roof. West front of brown brick with gable. Rusticated quoins. Arched entrance with brick quoins and keystone. Semi-circular fanlight. Blank window over. Brick band course."*

It was around 1728 when Colonel Martin Bladen built Aldborough House, fronting Oaks Lane and to the west of where St. Peter's stands today. This was a large mansion of red brick, costing £14,000, with two storeys and basements and ten windows across the front. The house was demolished shortly before 1808. The red-brick wall which today borders the south of St. Peter's Close and some of the gardens of the bungalows on the north side of Oaks Lane is thought to have survived from the garden of Col. Bladen's mansion. Parts of this wall and the wall at the rear of Lake Cottages *(see page 113)* may date back even further to Tudor times.

(Above) This wash drawing of Aldborough House and Chapel is in the Guildhall Library and is dated around 1800.

(Left) Part of the wall running at the rear of the gardens from 211 to 233 Oaks Lane, photographed from the north side in St. Peter's Close. The wall is Locally Listed by the London Borough of Redbridge.

The wall on the south side in a garden of a bungalow in Oaks Lane – by kind permission of Graham and Pat, who may have thought it a bit odd that I wished to point my camera at their garden wall but were too polite to say so! They told me it is Tudor and I believe them – whatever the pundits say.

The Locally Listed former Garden Wall at the rear of 211 to 233 Oaks Lane is the surviving north and west walls of the rectangular kitchen garden enclosure, probably a remnant of Aldborough House. It has been altered and rebuilt in parts and is 3.5 metres high where intact. It is built of plum-red bricks, mixed bond, predominantly Flemish, unbuttressed, tapering head terminated by brick on edge.

Aldborough Hatch Chapel was a small building, of red brick except for the east wall, which was of yellow brick: this wall was presumably built when the mansion was demolished. The parapet on the west, or entrance, front was lowered, destroying a former pediment. This front had brick quoins and a round-headed doorway with a 'Gibbs' surround and an original door. Since the mansion of circa.1728 had similar features, the west front of the Chapel probably dates from that time. In the 19th Century the Chapel had a gallery with high-backed pews, a tall pulpit and a covered pit just inside the door where lanterns could be left during services.

In her will dated 1746, Frances Bladen, wife of Colonel Bladen, left £20 a year, charged on her Aldborough Hatch estate, for a clergyman to officiate in her Chapel there. The Communion Plate was given in 1771. At the end of the 18th Century, the Chaplain was the Revd. Herbert Jeffries, BA. When the Aldborough Hatch estate was put up for sale in 1802 it was stipulated that the purchaser should continue the payment of £20. The Chapel was left standing when Aldborough House was demolished about 1808, and passed with the estate to the Crown in 1828. Services were continued there until 1863 when services started to be held in St. Peter's. In 1861, £20 was still being paid to the Chaplain, £3.3s to the Clerk, £2.2s to a pew-opener and £3 for other Chapel purposes (whatever they were and I am not one to speculate). Whilst £20 may not sound a princely sum to pay the Chaplain, it equates to around £12,000 in today's money (or so I am led to believe) and that probably kept him to a reasonable standard of living, with the occasional flagon of port (for medicinal purposes, of course!).

The Chapel from a water-colour, dated 1905, by Alfred Bennett Bamford (1857-1939) who was a topographical artist, living in nearby Romford for the earlier part of his life.

The Chapel showing the west wall – photographed in 1984. St. Peter's Church is in the distance to the left and the flats in St. Peter's Close are to the right.

By 1960, the Chapel was used as a farm building. The Vicar of St. Peter's tried to reclaim the Chapel from Ilford Council for use by the Rover Scout Crew – but all to no avail.
(Left) The west wall of the Chapel was blown down during the hurricane force winds on the night of 15th/16th October 1987.

After the building stood derelict and in danger of collapse, Redbridge Council leased the building for conversion into a private residence. The photograph (left) was taken in 2010. Conversion was completed in 2011 by Chartered Architect Balkrishna Savant, RIBA, FIIA, for his personal use.

The Chapel of St. James, Little Heath

St. James' Church, Little Heath.

In 1862 Major G. E. Ibbetson built a chapel – known as the Chapel of St. James – behind his residence at Heath House, Little Heath (on the corner where today the A12 meets Hainault Road as it rumbles into Essex). It was originally intended for the use of his family and friends, but it attracted a considerable congregation.

The chapel, seating 200, was never consecrated. It was built of brick, with stone dressings, and consisted of nave, chancel, aisles, transepts, and a west tower with five bells.

Major Ibbetson maintained it and employed a succession of curates until his death in 1908, when the Heath House estate was bought by the County Borough of West Ham for the extension of Goodmayes Mental Hospital. The chapel was leased by West Ham to the congregation. The last curate, the Revd. H. R. Landon, remained until 1918, when he moved to St. Alban's Church in Albert Road, Ilford. The Revd. Landon died in 1940 at the age of 82.

Financial difficulties in 1918 caused the congregation to appeal to the Bishop, who executed a new lease and placed the chapel under the administration of the Vicar of Aldborough Hatch, in whose parish it lay. Services were continued until about 1930.

In 1933 the building was demolished. What a tragedy! I would hope that would not be permitted to happen today. The brass processional cross, two chairs and the wood panelling in the sanctuary have been preserved in St. Peter's Church. These days the brass cross is carried in procession only at festivals at St. Peter's for it has developed a somewhat disturbing and alarming wobble and members of the congregation are prone to take cover as the crucifer moves stealthily down the aisle with the top of the cross waving threateningly aloft!

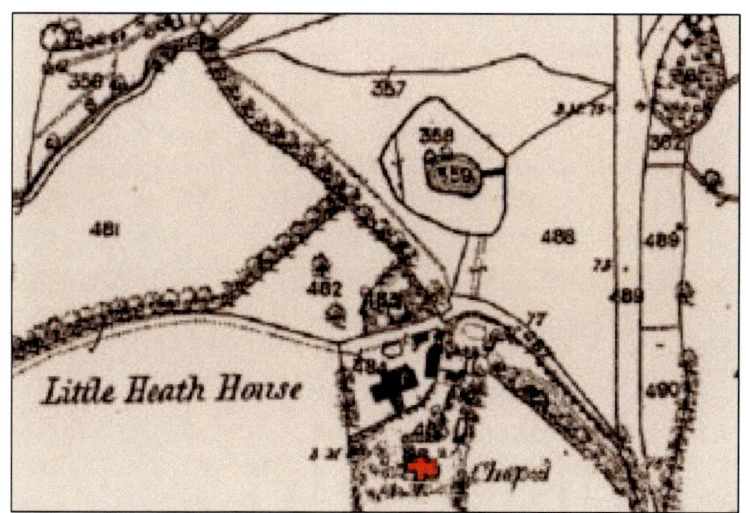

Ernest Ibbetson, born about 1830 in London, was a Lieutenant in the Hertfordshire Militia and Captain of 29th Middlesex Rifles, later a Major. He and his wife Frances lived at Heath House for many years and can be found in the 1861, 1871, 1881 censuses.

I am grateful to Gaby Laws of Genealogy Research Service for providing me with the following extract from *The Essex Standard and General Advertiser* of Wednesday 13th August 1862 reporting on the opening on 2nd August 1862 of what is described as the Little Heath Chapel, Chadwell – the Chapel of St. James:

"On the 2nd inst, a very unique little chapel was opened at Chadwell, near Ilford. It has been erected by the only gentleman in the neighbourhood, Captain Ibbetson, and has been built within his grounds under his personal superintendence, from his own plan as the work proceeded, and without the assistance of an architect.

"The Chapel, which is in the form of a patriarchal cross, has grown up under Captain Ibbetson's eye. His builder and labourers are all residents in the village and the work is very creditable to all parties concerned.

"The cost to this benefactor of his neighbourhood is little short of £2,000 and when it is considered there is no church within four miles – that several of the inhabitants in the village admitted that they have not been to church for years – no doubt can be entertained of its utility." (See next page.)

"The Hon. and Revd. Henry W. Bertie, DCL, Vicar of Great Ilford, commenced the morning prayer, the Revd. John Chittenden, the future minister, who has been for some years a missionary in Canada, read the first lesson, the Revd. George Martin Braune, formerly Vicar of Wistow, Yorkshire, read the second lesson, and the Revd. W. F. E. Knollys, incumbent of Barking Side, preached." (The Revd. Knollys was the first Vicar of St. Peter's Church, Aldborough Hatch, instituted in the following year, 1863 . . . see later.)

"The organist, Mr Dawson, and choir of Barking Church were in attendance and chanted the service. After the whole had been concluded the friends of Captain Ibbetson partook of an elegant cold collation in a marquee erected in his grounds, and a subscription list towards the future minister's stipend was passed round, when £60 was subscribed.

"After dinner the toasts of 'Her Majesty the Queen', 'The Prince of Wales and the rest of the Royal Family', 'The Bishop of the Diocese and the Clergy' were given by the gallant Captain, and the latter was responded to by the Hon. and Revd. Henry W. Bertie.

"The Revd. G. M. Braune proposed, in eulogistic terms, the 'Health of Captain and Mrs Ibbetson, and family', which was heartily received and warmly applauded. The evening was spent in rustic sports."

Reference is made in the above extract from the *The Essex Standard and General Advertiser* to the fact that *"several of the inhabitants of the village admitted they had not been to church for years"*. This may go some way to explaining the breach of Sunday trading laws at the Crooked Billet reported thus:

"There had been a public house at Padnall Corner from 1850. The innkeeper, Foster Threadgold, was summoned by the police at Ilford Petty Sessions for Sunday trading. The police reported that on Sunday 10th October 1858 at about a quarter to twelve o'clock, they entered the defendant's house by the back door and found five persons in the front room and six in the back room. They were all men and all were smoking and drinking. The defendant asked the Chairman: 'If I and my wife go to church on a Sunday morning whether the police are legally right in making a forcible entry into my house in my absence?' The Chairman answered: 'You must leave someone in charge of your premises to admit the police if necessary. I am very glad to hear of your going to church, but you are, no doubt guilty in this instance. You are fined the mitigated penalty of £3 and costs'."

And so the Chapel of St. James was opened in August 1862, but never consecrated. Meanwhile, a mile or so to the east in sunny Aldborough Hatch, St. Peter's Church had also been built and was consecrated on 6th March 1862 – the same year but five months earlier! And for that story please stay with us and read the next few pages – but there were no *"rustic sports"* at St. Peter's, whatever they were (and I think it best that we do not inquire any further into the matter for these things are often best left without investigation).

Westminster Bridge

The first Westminster Bridge, designed by Charles Labelage, was opened to traffic on 18th October 1750. The new Westminster Bridge was designed by Thomas Page in consultation with Sir Charles Barry, architect of the new Houses of Parliament, and was erected at a cost of £400,000. Building of the new bridge started in 1854. St. Peter's Aldborough Hatch was one of six churches in the London area built in Portland stone from the demolished 1750 bridge. In spite of exhaustive research (which can be exhausting) we have been unable to trace the other six (and we have looked – honest!). The stones were taken down river from Westminster on barges and may well have been unloaded on the River Roding at the point where Ilford Broadway stands today, to be brought by horse and cart to Aldborough Hatch. St. Peter's was consecrated on 6th March 1862.

Wordsworth wrote his *Ode to Westminster Bridge* whilst standing on the first Westminster Bridge.

> Earth has not anything to show more fair
> Dull would he be of soul who could pass by
> A sight so touching in its majesty:
> This City now doth like a garment wear
> The beauty of the morning; silent, bare,
> Ships, towers, domes, theatres, and temples lie
> Open unto the fields, and to the sky;
> All bright and glittering in the smokeless air.
> Never did sun more beautifully steep
> In his first splendour valley, rock, or hill;
> Ne'er saw I, never felt, a calm so deep!
> The river glideth at his own sweet will:
> Dear God! the very houses seem asleep;
> And all that mighty heart is lying still!

William Wordsworth (1770-1850)

The first Westminster Bridge under construction – 1740 (Canaletto)

The New Chapel at Aldborough Hatch

To appreciate what was going on with the building of St. Peter's we have to go back to 1838 when the movement for a new parish church at Barkingside began. A petition was sent to the Church Building Commissioners by inhabitants of Ilford, who promised to raise £1,000 for the purpose. The petition stated that the people of Barkingside were *"very destitute and degraded"* owing to the temptations to which they were exposed by the proximity of the forest, the nature of their occupations, and their visits to the London markets. All of which will probably come as something of a surprise to today's Barkingside residents – for I know many of them as personal friends and they seem to me to be honest, decent enough folk as they wander down the High Street and into Sainsbury's or Tesco. Things are probably best left there, for this book is aimed at a family market and we do not need to go into the details of the temptations of the forest, let alone how their occupations impinged on their lives, nor what happened when Barkingside folk visited the London markets! Such things are clearly not for the unsullied minds of my readers who I have a solemn duty to protect from such profanities.

The local landowners, who were non-resident, were said to take little interest in the inhabitants (more's the pity, I say). The only place of worship in the district was the private chapel at Aldborough Hatch – that which stands today on Aldborough House Farm. The Commissioners agreed to give £350 towards a church, and a site was given by the owners of Gayshams Hall. The building of t he church was completed in 1840, and in 1841 Barkingside became a district chapelry. The new benefice was a perpetual curacy, in the gift of the Vicar of Great Ilford. In addition to the money spent on building the church, £1,455 had been invested as an endowment, a tithe rent charge of £45 was allotted from the Vicarage of Great Ilford, and 20 acres of glebe were provided. The church of The Holy Trinity, Mossford Green, which stands in a graveyard, was designed by Edward Blore. It is a yellow-brick building in the 'Norman' style consisting of nave, chancel (added about 1895), and a north-west porch forming the base of a small tower with a spire. North and west vestries were added in the 20th century.

Under the *Hainault Forest Inclosure Act (1851)* land was set aside for the erection of a church for the new population expected in the district. In 1861 the Commissioners of Woods and Forests agreed to give £1,000 for a building that would take the place of the chapel at Aldborough Hatch, and promised that they would continue the annual payment of £20 towards the salary of the incumbent. In 1861/62 a church was built, and a district chapelry, taken from the parish of Holy Trinity, Barkingside, was formed. And thus St. Peter's Aldborough Hatch came into being! But why all this stuff about Holy Trinity? All will be revealed shortly.

The new benefice was endowed with a tithe rent charge of £25 from the Vicarage of Great Ilford, 3 acres of land valued at £350, and also the sum of £550. In 1865 the Commissioners added the further endowment of 11 acres of land, for which they agreed to pay an annuity of £21 13s. 4d. The church plate includes a cup, flagon, and alms dish of 1771, which came from the former chapel of Aldborough House. A large flagon and a paten at St. Peter's are inscribed: *"For use of the Chapel of Albro' Hatch in Essex"* and this could be the church plate referred to (note the spelling of *Albro'*). Following the 1851 Act of Parliament which 'disafforested' Hainault, 100,000 trees were felled on Crown land – as we recorded earlier. Large farms were laid out on the Fairlop Plain with housing for labourers. The initials 'VR' (Victoria Regina) in the brickwork of houses in Hainault and Forest Road – and other parts of Aldborough Hatch – remind us of the Crown connection. The Crown is the Patron of the living of St. Peter's.

So St. Peter's was born of the need for a church to serve the expected increase in the local population as farms replaced forest. The Crown gave the land and, as mentioned earlier, the Government gave £1,000 towards the cost of the church's erection, seen by many as atonement for the disafforestation, an act that – it is said – has never been forgiven.

At this time, the 18th Century Westminster Bridge in London was being replaced and the contractor also had the order for the new Church at Aldborough Hatch. Building of the new bridge started in 1854, but the old bridge was in use until the new one was nearing completion. The Portland stone of the old Westminster Bridge (supplied from the quarries on Portland Island in Dorset) was used to build St. Peter's – which was so named after the Collegiate Church of St. Peter at Westminster, popularly known as Westminster Abbey. There were plenty of bricks available for Ilford had its own brickfields, but no doubt it was cheaper to cart the stone from Westminster than to buy new bricks (and stone looks better, too!).

The architect was British architect, writer and artist Arthur Ashpitel (1807-1869). The son of architect William Hurst Ashpitel, he was born in Hackney and educated at Dr. Burnet's school in Hackney, until an accident crippled him for life. Trained by his father to the architect's profession, he set up on his own account in 1842. He built the churches of St. John's, Blackheath; St. Barnabas, Homerton; and St. Peter's Aldborough Hatch, as well as schools and private houses. In 1850 he entered into partnership with John Whichcord Jnr with whom he designed baths and washhouses at Swansea, Maidstone, Lambeth and elsewhere, and also churches, private houses, and the Ophthalmic Hospital and Kent Infirmary at Maidstone. They turned their attention to the improvement of dwellings for the labouring classes and, for a Committee, erected a block of dwellings for artisans at Lambeth. They promoted the idea of living in flats in a publication called *Town dwellings: an essay on the erection of fireproof houses in flats*. In 1853 Arthur Ashpitel left England in the company of David Roberts, RA, and lived for some time in Rome. An attack of malaria, suffered in Piedmont, further damaged his health. In 1855, he dissolved the partnership with John Whichcord, but continued to accept commissions. Following his Roman studies he exhibited two drawings at the Royal Academy and was a prolific writer who contributed to magazines and the transactions of learned societies. Arthur Ashpitel died on 18 January 1869 – seven years after St. Peter's was consecrated.

Built in 1861/62 in decorated Gothic style, St. Peter's has a steep pitch slate roof with small gable, louvered vents, a shingle spire, and an interior pitch pine roof.

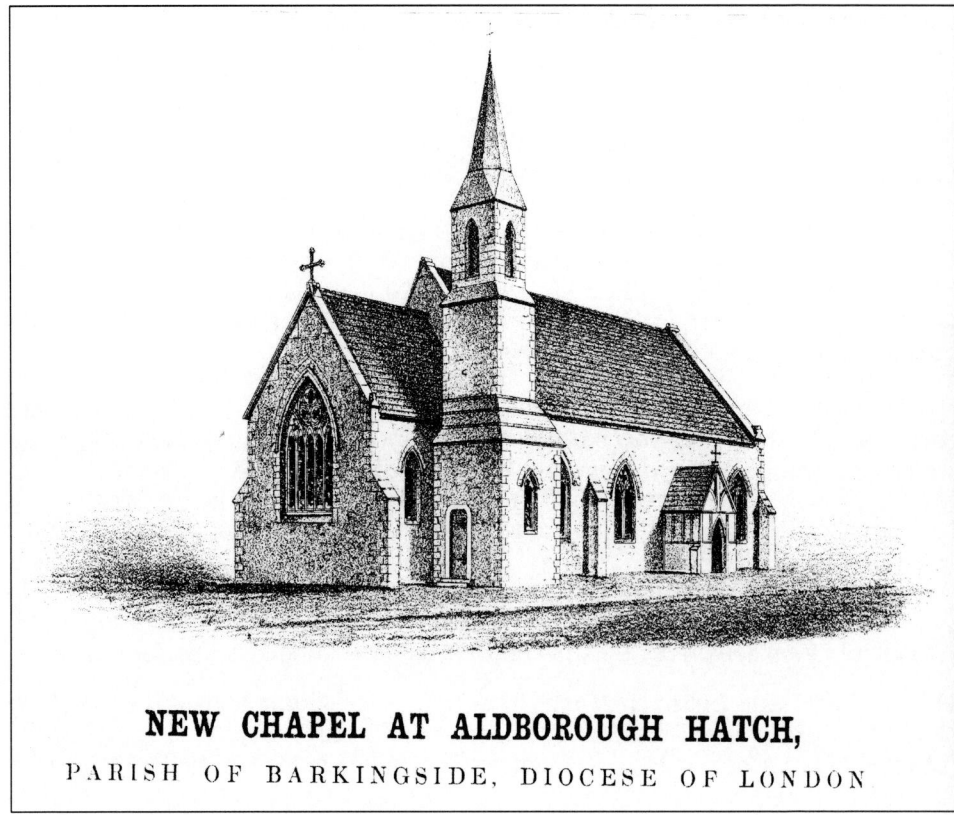

NEW CHAPEL AT ALDBOROUGH HATCH,
PARISH OF BARKINGSIDE, DIOCESE OF LONDON

Consecrated on 6th March 1862, it is Grade II Listed. An appeal leaflet was published, with an illustration showing the porch on the north side *(above);* when built the porch was on the south.

The leaflet *(see next page)* was for contributions to the building fund and to endow the new benefice. Commenting on the increased population expected, the leaflet states that: *"This increase is almost exclusively composed of the Labouring Classes..."* The names of the committee and donors are a social directory of the neighbourhood in the 1860s.

It is interesting that the architect of St. Peter's was concerned in his professional life to improve *"dwellings for the labouring classes"* and our church was built for a population *"almost exclusively composed of the Labouring Classes"*. As comedian Ronnie Corbett famously said: *"I know my place!"* and like Uriah Heep, I am the *"umblest person going"*.

Committee.

JOHN DAVIS, Esq. **Chairman.**

Hon. & Rev. H. W. BERTIE.
S. CHARRINGTON, Esq.
CHARLES GRAVES, Esq.

R. GLYNES, Esq.
W. HASLEHUST, Esq.
Rev. JOHN MEE.
S. MITCHELL, Esq.

J. PAULIN, Esq.
G. PAINTER, Esq.
Rev. J. REYNOLDS.

Rev. JOHN GODDING, **Secretary.**

The Committee of the New Chapel at Aldborough Hatch have the satisfaction of announcing, that the convenient and Ecclesiastical Edifice, now in course of erection, will be finished in the ensuing Summer; and they trust, that with the additional Subscriptions they still hope to receive, a sufficient sum will be obtained for its completion. They feel, however, that the time has now arrived for procuring such an Endowment as will permanently secure the services of a Clergyman in the New Church.

The population in the neighbourhood of the Chapel, will, by reason of the disafforesting of Hainault Forest, soon be double the number returned in the last census. This increase is almost exclusively composed of the Labouring Classes, and the Estates of the Crown being extensive, the District is deprived of the many advantages arising from resident Proprietors.

The Crown possesses the right of nominating a Minister to the Chapel; and has, through the Commissioners of Woods and Forests, made a liberal Grant towards the Building Fund. From the same source the sum of £20. is annually derived for the maintenance of Divine Worship.

It is proposed ultimately to attach a Parochial District to the Chapel, and the hope is entertained that the necessity for procuring an Endowment, in order that the accommodation in the Chapel may, for the most part, be appropriated to the Labouring Classes, will be recognized by those who desire to render, effective and permanent, this local effort to provide the Ministrations of the Church of England.

Donations will be thankfully received by MEMBERS OF THE COMMITTEE, or by the Bankers, MESSRS. DIMSDALE AND Co., 50, Cornhill. It is requested that when Contributions are paid to the Bankers, it may be stated whether the Donation is intended for the Building Fund, or the Endowment Fund. The following Amounts have already been received:—

Building Fund.

Crown, per Woods and Forests, Site and	£1000	- -
Incorporated Society	160	- -
Diocesan Society	100	- -
Lady Emily Bathurst	20	- -
John Davis, Esq.	25	- -
Hon. & Rev. H. W. Bertie	20	- -
Spencer Charrington, Esq.	20	- -
Samuel Mitchell, Esq.	20	- -
George Painter, Esq.	10	- -
Rev. John Mee	10	- -
W. Haslehust, Esq.	10	- -
James Paulin, Esq.	10	- -
Mrs. Verbeke	10	- -
	£1415	- -

Endowment Fund.

A Sum received in Compensation for an Injury sustained	£22 18 -

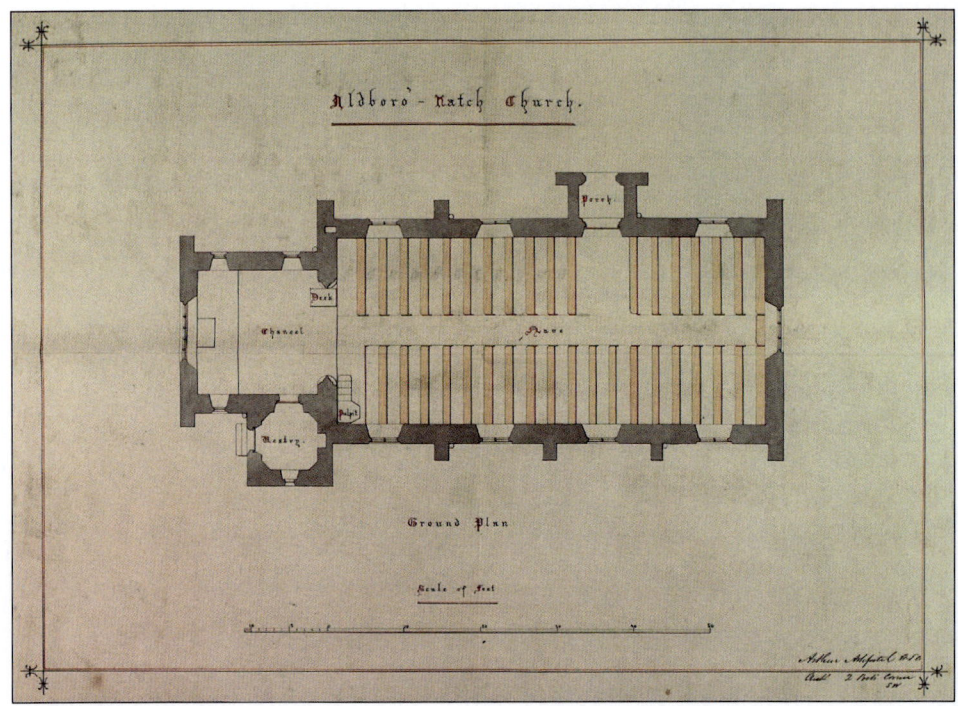

The Architect's ground plan dated 1860 for the Aldboro' Hatch Church (above), is held at Lambeth Palace Library (and published with permission), has a Vestry, Vicar's desk, pulpit, altar, but no choir stalls. There are 17 pews in the south aisle and 19 in the North aisle (total 35) said to seat 240. Today there are 11 on the south and 15 on the north (total 26) seating 130. In 1860 the church seated seven to a pew and today only five. Perhaps folk were thinner in Victorian England? Interestingly, Kelly's Directory of Essex 1895 says the church seated 300!

Evidence for the date of Consecration of St. Peter's is to be found on a silver paten amongst the Communion Plate, measuring some 8 inches in diameter with the following inscription: *"W F E K Incumbt. JMP curate A thank offering for the consecration of St. Peter's Church Aldborough Hatch March 6th 1862"*. The Revd. William Frederic Erskine Knollys was Vicar of Holy Trinity, Barkingside (1862 to 1864) and of St. Peter's (1863 to 1865). The Revd. John Mathias Proctor was Vicar of Holy Trinity (1864 to 1879) and of St. Peter's (1865 to 1879). The first Vestry Meeting at St. Peter's was held on 9th April 1863 where it is recorded that two Churchwardens were appointed *"one to be nominated by the Chaplain, till such time as the Incumbent be instituted and the other by the householders"*. The first Vicar took up his appointment more than a year after the Church was consecrated. Over the years numerous publications and many highly respected authors have stated – erroneously – that St. Peter's was consecrated in 1863, but we now have factual proof that the date was 6th March 1862.

The London Gazette and the Vicars of Aldborough Hatch

At this point it is instructive (well, I think so) to quote from that worthy publication, *The London Gazette*, which giveth (and you will note that I am into the lingo) a fascinating insight into 19th Century England in all matters ecclesiastical.

The London Gazette, 13th January 1863, page 195
At the Court at Osbourne House, Isle of Wight, the 9th day of January, 1863.
Present: The Queen's Most Excellent Majesty in Council
"We, the Ecclesiastical Commissioners for England" make *"the following representation as to the assignment of a consolidated chapelry to the consecrated church of Saint Peter, situate at Aldborough Hatch, in the new parish of Trinity, Barkingside, in the county of Essex, and in the diocese of London. Whereas at certain extremities of the said new parish of Trinity, Barkingside, and of the parish of Great Ilford . . . there is collected together a population which is situate at a distance from the several churches . . . it appears to us to be expedient that such contiguous portions of the said new parish of Trinity, Barkingside, and of the said parish of Great Ilford, should be formed into a consolidated chapelry for all ecclesiastical purposes and that the same should be assigned to the said church of Saint Peter, situate at Aldborough Hatch aforesaid."*

The text runs over two pages setting out the boundaries of the parish of St. Peter's *"by an imaginary line . . . at a point in the middle of Oaks-lane, opposite to the middle of the south-eastern end of a certain lane leading to Lover's-walk . . . "* Later there is reference to *"Craw brook"* (the Cranbrook stream), *"Aldborough Hatch Gate", "Maypole Gate", "Hoghill", "Forest Farm", "Chadwell-street", "Chadwell Heath", "Aldborough Hatch-lane"* and *"Newbury Farm"* before we return to *"Oaks-lane"* but not, you will be saddened to read, to *"Lover's-walk"*. But where was *"Lover's-walk"*? Sadly, my research has drawn a blank, but I like to think it was that spot we know today as Chase Lane, with Oaks Park High School and the recreation ground on one side and the fields of Aldborough Hatch Farm on the other, leading to the bridge over the Central Line and onwards to Sainsbury's. A map was said to be *"thereunto annexed"* but I have been unable to trace this.

Furthermore, Her Majesty *"was pleased, by and with the advice of Her Privy Council, to approve thereof; and to order . . . the presentation and appointment of an incumbent or perpetual curate to serve the said church . . . and that the said right of presentation and appointment . . . shall belong to and be exercised by Her Majesty and Her successors in right of the Crown; and Her Majesty is further pleased to direct that this Order be forthwith registered by the Registrar of the diocese of London."* All of which is signed by one Arthur Helps.

And so you will see that St. Peter's is to have not only an incumbent, but a perpetual curate, which means that we are a Crown Living and that the Monarch presents and appoints an incumbent. And that incumbent is a Vicar, for **The London Gazette, 31st August 1866, page 4801** states *"to all to whom these* *presents shall come, we, the Ecclesiastical Commissioners for England, send greeting . . . acting in pursuance of The District Church Tithes Act, 1865 do hereby declare . . . the said church of the consolidated chapelry of Saint Peter, Aldborough Hatch aforesaid, shall be deemed to be a vicarage."*

So enamoured are we with the language that we just have to quote the following:
The London Gazette, 11th April, 1902, page 2416
"Crown Office – 10th April, 1902
"THE KING" (their capitals, not mine) *"has been pleased, by Letters Patent under the Great Seal, to present the Reverend Philip Isidore Lach-Szyrma, M.A., to the Vicarage of Aldborough Hatch, in the county of Essex, and diocese of St. Albans, void by the death of the Reverend Charles Edward Lathbury, the last Incumbent, and in His Majesty's Gift in full right."* And there are similar entries for later Vicars.

St. Peter's started life in the Diocese of London, but in 1875 the church moved into the new diocese of St. Albans – where it stayed until 1914 when the new diocese of Chelmsford was created, removing Essex from the St. Albans diocese. I dislike correcting a fellow author, especially one who is long deceased, but in *Ilford Past and Present,* George Tasker states that until 1877 Ilford was in the Diocese of Rochester, whereas the **London Gazette, 13th January 1863**, page 195 records that St. Peter's and Trinity were both in the Diocese of London.

Incumbents of St. Peter's, Aldborough Hatch from 1863 to date:

1863: Revd. W. F. Erskine Knollys
1865: Revd. John Mathias Proctor
1879: Revd. Charles S. Chilver
1885: Revd. Henry W. H. Bircham
1886: Revd. C. E. Lathbury
1902: Revd. Philip Lach-Szyrma
1931: Revd. Joseph Palanque Byng
1951: Revd. Lawrence E. Pickles
1962: Revd. John Jack Hesketh
1966: Revd. William A. C. Barnes
1983: Revd. John Fulton
1987: Revd. Michael J. Trodden
1997: Revd. Tim Coleman
2003: Revd. Clare Nicholson
2012: Revd. Kate Lovesey

Incumbents of Holy Trinity, Barkingside from consecration in 1840 to date:

1840: Revd. John Budgen
1862: Revd. W. F. Erskine Knollys
1864: Revd. John Mathias Proctor
1879: Revd. Thomas Andrew Walker
1885: Revd. Alban Wyld
1886: Revd. Thomas Norwood Perkins
1890: Revd. Wladislaw Somerville Lach-Szyrma
1915: Revd. Charles John Wills
1923: Revd. Albert Morris Wheatley
1950: Revd. John Stokes Newman
1967: Revd. Christopher Reeves
1997: Revd. Brian Maurice Branche
2005: Revd. Edmund Alwyn James Cargill Thompson
2014: Revd. Stuart Batten

It would appear that for the first sixteen years of its existence, St. Peter's, Aldborough Hatch, shared its Vicar with Trinity, Barkingside (more recently known as Holy Trinity). It is probable that the first two Vicars lived in Barkingside, for the Vicarage at St. Peter's was not built at the same time as the church, but some sixteen years later around 1879 or 1880. How did the Vicar travel to conduct services – did he walk or have a pony and trap? We may never know.

Sadly – and in spite of fervent efforts – we cannot trace photographs of the first five Vicars of St. Peter's, which is a pity for they were no doubt handsome fellows. The Revd. Phillip Lach-Szyrma *(left)* – Vicar from 1902 – was the son of the Revd. Wladislaw Somerville Lach-Szyrma MA, FRHS, who was born at Devonport on 25th December 1841. His father, Krystyn Lach-Szyrma, a Polish Professor, moved from Warsaw c1830 to escape persecution (at the time of the November Uprising), and married into the naval Somerville family in Plymouth. After studying the classics at Brasenose College, Oxford, his first curacy was at Pensilva. In 1869 he took the curacy of St Paul's, Truro, and Carnmenellis in 1871. On his return from Paris, after a short illness (and his obituary published in a number of newspapers!), he became the Vicar of St. Peter's Church, Newlyn from 1873 until 1890. He then moved to Holy Trinity, Barkingside, where he died in 1915. He was a prolific writer on church history and the antiquities of Cornwall, especially of the district around Penzance and was also a pioneer of science-fiction. Thus father Wladislaw and son Phillip served for some 13 years in neighbouring parishes – and both were Oxford men.

The Revd. Joseph Palanque Byng, (1931) with the St. Peter's Choir, 1950. (Back row) Tony Mathews (Server), 'Mr T' (Lay Reader), Mr Cornish, Ron Jeffries (Server), Mr Bretton (Choirmaster), Mr Smith, Mr Webb, Mr Vernon, Colin Brett, Mr Fairey (Organist), Brian Brett (Server). (Middle row) Ted Vernon, Geoff Griffiths (Server), Bob Smith, Raymond Woolmore, Adrian Lankaster, Brenda Harmer. (Front row) Lawrence Tasker, John Bretton, Barry Priest, Brian Heaton. Yvonne Jeffries (neé Friend) joined in 1951.

(Above left) Revd. Lawrence Pickles (1951) – a newspaper journalist prior to ordination.
(Above right) Revd. John Jack Hesketh (1962) – a chaplain to the deaf before coming to St. Peter's.
(Left) Far right – Revd. William (Bill) Barnes (1966) with Archie Titmarsh (known affectionately as 'Mr T') Reader, Group Scout Leader and Sunday School teacher.

(Right) From left to right – Vicars all – Tim Coleman (1997), Clare Nicholson (2003), Michael Trodden (1987) and John Fulton (1983) at the 30th Flower Festival in 2010. I will say only that they were good folk – which they were – who served us well.

Churchwardens of Aldborough Hatch

Year	Incumbent's/Vicar's Warden	Parishioners'/People's Warden
1863/65	Captain Ibbetson	George Painter
1866	George Painter	Mr Davis
1867	George Painter	William Reynolds
1868	George Painter	Mr Hamilton
1869/71	George Painter	Mr Shacklady
1872	Alfred Harrison	Mr Shacklady
1873/75	Alfred Harrison	George Painter
1876	Alfred Harrison	J. H. Swift
1877/78	Charles Painter	Mr Shacklady
1879	Charles Painter	Isaac Lake
1880/83	Alfred Harrison	Isaac Lake
1884/85	Mr Earley	Isaac Lake
1886	Mr Earley	Charles Painter
1887/93	Mr Earley	Charles Painter
1894	Captain Amos	Charles Painter
1895/98	Mr Cardoza	Charles Painter
1899/02	C. Church	Charles Painter
1903/14	Charles James Painter	Isaac Lake
1915/16	Bessie Painter	Isaac Lake
1917	F.S. Fawcett	Isaac Lake
1918/23	F. S. Fawcett	W. A. Porter
1924/32	W. S. Torbitt	W. A. Porter
1933/34	Mr Jenvey	Mr Melbourne
1935	Mr Jenvey	Mr Bennett
1936/40	Mr Jenvey	Mr Allies
1941	Mr Jenvey	A. Walters
1942	A. J. Walters	Mr Prior
1943/44	A. J. Walters	J. W. Cooper
1945/48	J. W. Cooper	Mr Sewell
1949/54	J. W. Cooper	Mr George
1955/58	J. W. Cooper	Cyril Lewis
1959/60	Cyril Lewis	Cliff Wareing
1961	Cyril Lewis	Stanley Irons
1962/64	Cyril Lewis	Cliff Wareing
1965	George Woodcock	John DeBere (Acting)
1966	Gilbert Linsdell	Vacant
1967	Gilbert Linsdell	Stanley Irons
1968/71	Alan George Padfield	Stanley Irons
1972/74	Alan George Padfield	John DeBere
1975	Alan George Padfield	James Jock Mugford
1979/84	Richard Quennell Lewis (Dick)	James Jock Mugford
1985/88	Richard Quennell Lewis (Dick)	Derek Smith
1989/97	Lucy Allison	Derek Smith
1998	Sue Paddon	Derek Smith
1999/03	Sue Paddon	Roger Towler
2004	Sue Paddon	Roger Goffee
2005/09	Roger Goffee	Martyn Stewart

2010	Chris Kerrison	Martyn Stewart
2011	Chris Kerrison	Roger Kirby
2016	Glenn Harvey	Roger Kirby
2017	Glenn Harvey	Lee Hawkes

Churchwardens are elected at the Annual Vestry Meeting, today held in April or May, but in the past as early as January. At first these meetings were held in the Vestry Room which was probably in the church, either the area under the bell tower (which we call today the Vicar's Vestry) or a curtained-off area at the rear north-west corner of the church (which was used as the choir vestry, housing the choir robes, from the time I joined the choir in 1944 until the Vestry was built as part of the Church Hall extension in 1958). The Minutes record that the Vestry Meetings from 1863 to the end of the century were attended by the Vicar and two or three others – often both Churchwardens and one other. Churchwardens were called Incumbent's Warden and Parishioners' Warden until 1886 when the present designations of Vicar's Warden and People's Warden were adopted.

At the Vestry Meeting in 1915 it is recorded that *"The Vicar feelingly alluded to the great loss the Parish had recently sustained by the death of Mr Charles James Painter . . . friend and benefactor"*. (I have to say that no-one has ever *"feelingly alluded"* to me, but then I remain alive.) The Vicar then nominated Mrs Bessie Painter, Charles Painter's widow, as Vicar's Warden, who *"graciously accepted the Office"*. Thus Mrs Painter was the first woman Churchwarden at St. Peter's – which is remarkable in view of the fact that women were denied the vote at the time. It would be three years later – in 1918 – when the franchise was extended to women over the age of 30 and not until 1928 when universal suffrage was achieved for all adults over the age of 21. Two years later in 1917 it was noted in the Minutes that Mrs Painter had *"removed from the Parish"* and the connection with the Painter family was thus severed after 54 years.

Following the death of Isaac Lake, his widow was nominated as People's Warden at the Vestry Meeting in 1918, but *"Mrs Lake, while deeply appreciating the honour proposed, felt bound to decline to stand"*. And so St. Peter's had to wait another 71 years until 1989 for another woman to be nominated as Churchwarden, when Lucy Allison stepped into the fray, followed by Sue Paddon and Chris Kerrison. But equally fascinating is that at a meeting of the Parochial Church Council on 9th May 1965, it was agreed that ladies might be appointed *"as sidesmen with the gentlemen"* and *"After some discussion, on the proposition of Mr Berry, seconded by Miss Lane and with one abstainer* (I wonder who he was!), *it was agreed that the office of People's Warden should be open to a lady or gentleman. Nominations were then invited but as none was forthcoming the Vicar undertook to explain to the Archdeacon that certain changes were in mind and no People's Warden had as yet been appointed. It was therefore decided to defer the matter for discussion at the meeting of the Council convened for 20th May. In the meantime the Council was asked to pray for guidance in approaching nominees."* Little did those good folk know that a lady had been appointed as Vicar's Warden fifty years earlier. Pity they were too busy discussing, debating, proposing, seconding – and abstaining – and did not take time out to check previous Minutes!

St. Peter's Vicarage

(Above and left) St. Peter's Vicarage in the 30s and 40s when the Revd. Byng was Vicar.

The first Vicarage stood on the corner of Oaks Lane, slightly back from the present Vicarage. The lawn ran from the house to the first bungalow on the west side of Oaks Lane. The original Vicarage was built later than the Church – in 1879 or thereabouts – and, as we surmised earlier, the first two Vicars may have lived in Barkingside. The Minute Book of Parochial and Vestry Meetings from 1863 records that these meetings were initially held in the Vestry Room but in the Minute for the Vestry Meeting on 9th May 1887 it is clearly stated that the Vicar and two local worthies met in the Vicarage. The ensuing Vestry Meetings were held in the Vestry Room until 10th April 1890 when the Minutes read: *"At the suggestion of the Vicar, the meeting was adjourned to the Vicarage"*. With one coal, coke and wood stove for heating, the church was almost certainly very cold and perhaps there was some warming liquor to be had at the Vicarage – a building which in itself was renowned for being extremely cold. My contemporaries and I recall sitting through Confirmation Classes conducted by the Revd. Byng in the Vicarage in the 1940s in the depths of winter, shivering and with teeth chattering!

The Vicarage was demolished in 1965 when the Revd. Jack Hesketh – who, in his capacity as incumbent held the title deeds of the Vicarage, very large garden and meadow – with the agreement of the Crown Land Commissioners, sold the garden and meadow to a builder for housing for £82,500. This sum was invested for the benefit of the Vicar for the time being, the Revd. Hesketh – which had the effect of producing one of the highest stipends in the Diocese – higher, it was said, than the Bishop himself! Sadly, the Revd. Hesketh died suddenly at the end of 1965 and only had the benefit of this stipend for a few months and never occupied the new Vicarage (which was erected as part of the deal with the builders). Shortly after the Revd. Bill Barnes was appointed Vicar in 1966 the Diocese adjusted the Vicar's stipend to a figure more in keeping with the Diocesan average. This is recorded in *The London Gazette*, 8th August 1967, page 8720, as follows: *"Pursuant to the Pastoral Reorganisation Measure, 1949, the Church Commissioners hereby give notice that they have made an Order dated the 3rd day of August 1967 to take effect as from 1st September 1967 and diverting to the diocesan stipends funds of the diocese of Chelmsford part of the endowment income of the benefit of Aldborough Hatch, St. Peter in the said diocese of Chelmsford."* When church law changed in the 1970s, the stipend reverted to be the same as that for other clergy – and I would assume that the Diocese took the balance of the endowment into their coffers. And so except for a short time neither subsequent Vicars, nor the Parish, benefited financially from the sale of the land – despite assurances given to the Parochial Church Council at the time. The only real benefit was that later incumbents have lived in a modern Vicarage where the icy winds did not blow through ill-fitting windows and doors, and the floorboards did not creak eerily on windy nights! But sadly, the Parish lost a very fine garden and meadow where the Scouts and Guides spent happy evenings and weekends, camping under the stars and singing round the camp fire, and where the locals enjoyed fétes and garden parties on summer days – when the sun always shone, warm and bright. My personal view is that the loss of the fine Victorian Vicarage and the open land to the parish was a tragedy of massive proportions that should never have been allowed to happen – and in all probability would not be permitted today when we are more concerned to preserve buildings of historic interest and conserve the Green Belt, of which the land was surely part. At the time the decision by the Vicar (with, I assume, the connivance of the Diocese) split the church into two factions and there were resignations – but it is in the past now and best forgotten (and to be much regretted). The flats and maisonettes of St. Peter's Close were built on the land, and many families have lived happily there on the edge of the Green Belt of Fairlop Plain looking out to Fairlop Waters Country Park . . . of which more later.

(Left) Favell Byng, daughter of Revd. and Mrs Byng, with David Greer, who served with the Ulster Rifles based locally during the 1939-45 World War, sitting on a gate leading to the Vicarage meadow in the early 1940s.

(Left - from left to right) The Revd. Joseph Palanque Byng, Mrs Doris Byng, Favell and David Greer – David is holding their daughter, Carole (now Carole Holme) circa 1949. Their first child, David, drowned in the Vicarage Lake in 1949 – see page 59.

(Left) Favell was named after her godmother, Favell Mary (nee Hill), Lady Miles, who was the novelist wife of Sir Charles William Miles, 5th Bt, and the daughter of Charles Gathorne Hill – a portrait of Lady Miles by Bassano dated 1919 is in the National Portrait Gallery. Favell, who died in 1972, aged only 48, and David dedicated their lives to caring for children and for ten years prior to her death Favell was matron of a home for children with both physical and learning disabilities. David continued with his day job but the family all lived in the home and were very much part of the daily activities. David died in 1996. Daughter Carole lives in Loughborough, where she is a textile artist (see www.caroleholme.co.uk). Having retired from St. Peter's to live in Southbourne, the Revd. Joseph Palanque Byng died in 1970 and Mrs Byng in 1977.

The Vicarage lake at the time when Revd. Byng was Vicar. The lake stretched from the garden to the far end of the meadow – the length of today's St. Peter's Close. The Vicarage roof is seen at the extreme left and the Tudor wall (still there today) is on the extreme right.

The lake where it joined the Vicarage garden. The gate on the left led into the meadow. The figure standing in the summerhouse may be the Revd. Byng. When the lake was to be filled in so that the housing in St. Peter's Close could be built in the 60s, there was concern amongst the angling community as to the many fish that inhabited the lake. Elsie Briscoe tells me that her son, Rex and his fishing friends, hired a lorry and filled dustbins with the fish which were then transported to the lake at Hainault Forest.

The Vicarage Garden Party, June 1951. The author and Yvonne Friend (who married in 1957) – stand behind the Fancy Dress Parade. Seventh from left in the parade (dressed as the King of Hearts) is the Revd. Lawrence Pickles' nephew (who had the look of someone sucking marbles!). Fourth from the left is Ken Paul (Robin Hood) whilst on his left is Margaret Paul (now Margaret Arden) – children of Norman and the redoubtable Una Paul. We cannot identify the bored – and yawning – nurse or the elegant young drummer boy, but Adrian Lankaster is the Scout in uniform to my right. Adrian's father and mother were pillars of St. Peter's. Adrian subsequently became Scout Borough Commissioner for Poole in Dorset.

(Left) The Revd. Pickles canoeing on the Vicarage Lake in the late 1950s – his mother on the bank. He would often garden in the nude and visitors were warned by his mother to call out as they walked down the garden!

The Meadow during a Vicarage Garden Party in the 1950s or early 60s with the 1st Aldborough Hatch (St. Peter's) Scout Group running sideshows. The houses in Oaks Lane – built in the late 1940s – are seen in the background, with Aldborough House Farm. (Inset) 'Mr T', Group Scout Leader, on the Vicarage Lawn, with Peter Dearlove in tartan shirt.

The Vicarage – built in the 1960s, seen in 2011. The low-level building on the left houses the hall, study and parish office (the latter may also be entered from outside).

St. Peter's Aldborough Hatch over the years

ALDBOROUGH HATCH — CHURCH

This postcard of St. Peter's, postmarked 22nd June 1905, is reproduced by kind permission of John Whitworth (www.essexchurches.info). The noticeboard, with a wooden cross at the top and standing above the hedgerow, includes a Notice of Election in the Borough of Ilford. The walls are covered by dense climbing foliage, which almost certainly would have eaten into the stonework and mortar. By 2004 much of the exterior stonework was crumbling and had to be replaced with Portland stone, whilst a special mortar mix was used – all at a cost in excess of £32,000, which was raised locally and through an appeal to trusts.

This postcard is postmarked 8th October 1906 with the legend 'Aldborough Hatch' at the bottom left hand corner. Can we discern the outline of the west wall of St. Peter's in the trees on the far right – or am I imagining something that is not there? If it is, this could be the Vicarage meadow.

This postcard is postmarked Ilford, 29th August 1928. There is no pavement and the walls of the church are covered in a heavy creeper, possibly ivy. The pipe sticking up through the roof towards the rear is the chimney from a stove that heated the church – planks on the inside of the roof show cuts where the chimney passed through.

St. Peter's Church, Aldborough Hatch   No. 435

I thank Carole Holme, granddaughter of the Revd. Byng, for these photographs. The first probably dates from the 1930s when some ivy remained on the walls; the second may date from the late 1930s or 1940s. Did a Churchwarden own the limousine which is purring into the photograph from the left? The road sign above the hedge reads Aldboro Road – nowadays it is Aldborough Road North.

This line drawing – signed RJW – appeared on the front cover of the St. Peter's Yearbook 1958-1959.

This much-loved line drawing by the late Frank Hebbard, who lived with his family in Aldborough Road North, has been used on St. Peter's BROADSHEET and NOTICESHEET, cards and stationery, since it was drawn in the 1980s. Frank's watercolours (see next page) may be seen in homes both in Aldborough Hatch and further afield for he was a prolific artist, selling his work at local events.

Frank Hebbard led an art group at St. Peter's in the 1980s and 1990s, and painted many watercolours of the church. This one is dated 1989.

This line drawing, probably dated to the 1980s, is by Mr Smith, who lived in Bawdsey Avenue with his wife and son, Bob, who was a member of St. Peter's Church Choir in the 1940s and 1950s. Mr and Mrs Smith were members of St. Peter's before moving into Essex to retire, where Mr Smith sketched many churches in the county.

St. Peter's Church, Wednesday 24th January 2007. The signpost is for Bridleway 93 – leading to Oaks Lane (1/4 mile) and Barkingside (3/4 mile).

St. Peter's Church, Wednesday 24th January 2007 (it was mighty cold that morning) from Aldborough Road North over Aldborough Hatch Farm.

In October 2015 some 2,500 Tête-à-tête Narcissus (daffodil to you and me) were planted between the main gate and the porch, and more the following year.

The footpath to the Aldborough Hall Equestrian Centre with protective wooden posts – installed by the Council following concern over pedestrian safety.

Aldborough Church School and Church Halls

In 1867 Aldborough Hatch Church of England School was built. The Architect was G. R. Clarke. An engraved stone below the eaves reads: *"Her Majesty Queen Victoria granted the site and £200 towards the building of this school erected to the Glory of God and to the use of the poor of Aldborough Hatch"*. The school was built to accommodate 160 boys and girls – they must have been slim! In 1893, this was one of five elementary schools within the boundary of the Ilford School Board. In 1895 the average attendance was 135. The original building can be traced – it comprised two rooms beneath the pitched roofs which stand today. It was a simple structure – a slate-covered dual-pitch roof and walls of local yellow stock bricks, with corbelling to gables and eves, and flat arches to the original gable windows. On the north elevation a cross in the brickwork denotes where the school bell once hung, but who took it and when – and where is it now?

St. Peter's Church and Church of England School from a postcard postmarked 1906. The schoolmaster's cottage on the far left was the Verger's home until the 1960s. It was demolished when unsafe in the 1970s. The postcard was sent by May Featherstone of Selborne Road, Ilford. May was born in 1883 in West Ham. The 1901 Census shows her as an 18-year-old bookbinder. May was 23 years old in 1906 when she sent this postcard to her Uncle Will in Halstead. William John Featherstone lived at 19 Chapel Street, Halstead. He was born in Woodford in 1850. The 1901 Census shows him as 51-years-of-age. He was 56 when he received the postcard of St Peter's from May Featherstone. In the 1911 Census William Featherstone is shown as aged 61 – "Retired Coachman".

This undated postcard shows an area in front of the school enclosed with a fence with barbed wire on the churchyard side, but not on the frontage to the road. There is a barbed wire enclosure behind the fence on the left hand side with what could be shrubs or roses. The church wall to the left of the porch is covered in ivy or a similar climber. When the postcard was bought on eBay in 2011, both the author and Pat had a recollection of the wooden fence in their youth in the 1940s.

Taken in 2011, this shows some of the grave stones that appear in the above postcard. These are dated variously 1905, 1907, 1908 and 1909. The White cross in the background in front of the East wall is on a grave dated 1911. For this reason we would date the postcard (top) circa 1910 to 1912.

The School was closed in 1912 when the building was adapted for use as St. Peter's Church Halls. The site of the Church Halls was purchased from the Crown Land Commissioners in 1948 for £50, one condition being that the land is vested in the Diocesan Board of Finance and the Parochial Church Council subject to the latter body maintaining fully the Caretaker's Cottage (which was later demolished!) and the hall for Sunday School purposes: failure to maintain these adequately would mean that the Parochial Church Council ceased to have any rights and the Crown had the immediate option of reclaiming them for £50. The Church Halls were extended in 1958 at a cost of £4,714.14s.5d when two flat-roofed structures (which have been a problem ever since!) were added – the large Hall fronting onto Aldborough Road North and the Vestry Room on the north-west corner. The smaller of the two schoolrooms was divided into an entrance hall, a kitchen, and toilets. The Headquarters of the 1st Aldborough Hatch (St. Peter's) Scout Group was added and opened on 3rd February 1979. The building of the former school is Locally Listed by the London Borough of Redbridge.

The Organ at St. Peter's

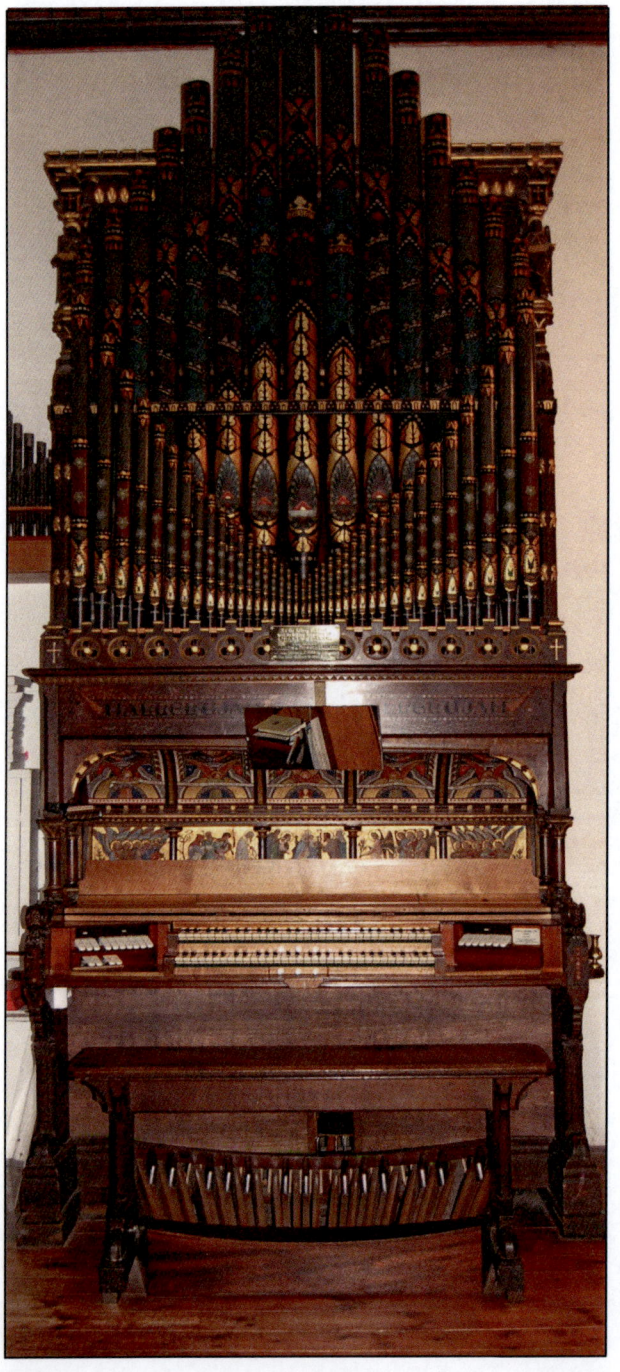

Prior to the acquisition of the organ there was little if any provision at St. Peter's for music – yet in the accounts for the year ended Easter 1871, £5 was *"paid for choir instruction"*, £1.0s.9d for *"washing surplices"* and 18s for *"hiring harmonium"*. The organ at St. Peter's was built by Gray and Davison Ltd (established 1862) for the 1862 London Exhibition, held in the gardens of the Royal Horticultural Society: the Science Museum now stands on this site. It is said that the organ was later installed in a public house in London's East End, before being acquired by Charles and Bessie Painter of Aldborough Hall, who presented the organ to St. Peter's in 1898 in memory of their son, Charles Alec, who died on 11th February 1893 aged six months. Herbert Freshwater was appointed organ blower at £1.10s per annum in 1898, for the organ was hand-pumped until 1951. The organ was rebuilt and enlarged by Gray and Davison in 1958, when a second manual was added and pipework replaced. The cost was covered by legacies of Miss Eliza C Babbs, Miss Jane Hoy and

Miss Ada Dawson, and gifts of the Vicar and congregation. A Service of Rededication of the Organ was held on 20th April 1958 with a recital by J. H. Sowerbutts of the Royal College of Music. Restoration in 1994 cost £17,500 and in 1999 two stops were installed coupling the big pedal to the great and swell manuals. An electronic piano was purchased in 1999 for use in church and halls.

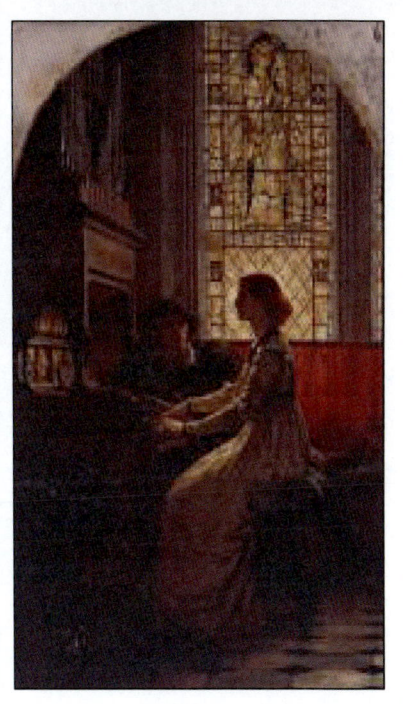

(Above left) The pipes – richly treated in mainly blues and yellows. (Above right) One of the painted panels above the keyboard depicting angels. The organ was the model for the painting 'Harmony' (left) by Sir Frank Dicksee (1853-1928) which hangs in the Tate Gallery. The painting is dated 1877, 16 years before the organ was installed at St. Peter's. The stained glass window in the painting is not in St. Peter's and it is said that the organ was in a public house in London's East End when this painting was completed. A print of the painting may be seen at the side of the organ.

The decoration on the organ was painted and stencilled by Nathaniel Hubert John Westlake (1833-1921), a British artist specialising in stained glass. He began to design for the firm of Lavers & Barraud, Ecclesiastical Designers, in 1858, became a partner ten years later and sole proprietor in 1880, when the firm was known as Lavers & Westlake. A leading designer of the Gothic Revival movement and a Catholic convert, his works include stained glass for Arundel Cathedral. In 1872 he painted the Reredos for the Roman Catholic Church of St. Charles Borromeo in London – composed of ten panels depicting the Crucifixion on violet brown coloured slates, probably from the Delabole Quarry in Cornwall.

BY APPOINTMENT

TO H.M. THE QUEEN   ORGAN BUILDERS

WM HILL & SON AND NORMAN & BEARD LTD.

ST. PETER'S PARISH CHURCH – ALDBOROUGH HATCH

This delightful instrument was built by Messrs Gray & Davison during the middle of the last century for the Great Exhibition. Sir Frank Dicksee used this organ as a model for his painting "Harmony". This painting was purchased by Chantry bequest and now hangs in the Tate Gallery.

In its original form, the instrument was of one manual with a lower octave of Bourdons permanently coupled to the keyboard. The original specification would have been an unenclosed Open Diapason 8ft and three enclosed stops being Stopped Diapason 8ft, Dulciana 8ft and Flute 4ft, plus the 12 Bourdon pipes.

To improve the instrument's use for congregational singing it was decided in 1957 to enlarge the instrument to a 2 manual with pedal using the extension principle; this was fairly successful considering the budget at the time.

Our company has been commissioned to undertake the necessary work needed to restore this instrument to first-class working order, which will include the total replacement of the 1957 electric action.

The current specification is as follows:-

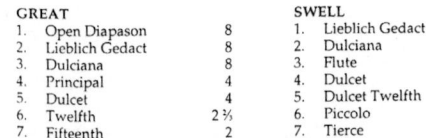

GREAT			SWELL			PEDAL		
1.	Open Diapason	8	1.	Lieblich Gedact	8	1.	Bourdon	16
2.	Lieblich Gedact	8	2.	Dulciana	8	2.	Open Diapason	8
3.	Dulciana	8	3.	Flute	4	3.	Bass Flute	8
4.	Principal	4	4.	Dulcet	4	4.	Principal	4
5.	Dulcet	4	5.	Dulcet Twelfth	2⅔	5.	Flute	4
6.	Twelfth	2⅔	6.	Piccolo	2			
7.	Fifteenth	2	7.	Tierce	1⅗			

The Manor Works, Orange Street, Thaxted, Essex CM6 2LH
Tel: 0371 830338/830827 Fax: 0371 831225

The Sculpture: *And other sheep I have* – Anthony Foster

Et alias oves hab eo (And other sheep I have: St. John, Chapter 10, vv 16) is the title of the sculpture in St. Peter's, which was acquired in 1959 by the then Vicar, Revd. Lawrence Pickles. For many years the sculpture stood on the shelf in front of the World War I War Memorial, but in 2011 a new oak shelf was commissioned, where it is displayed today *(left)*.

The sculptor was Anthony Noel Henry Foster (1909-1957). Anthony Foster was an unassuming man, who never sought fame and died at the early age of 49. However, he was a sculptor of great skill and his work was of high quality. He was also a deep-thinking man and a devout Catholic with a sincere love for his fellow-men.

He was born in Patna in India in 1909, the son of a High Court Judge under the British Raj. Anthony came back to school in England and his last school was Downside Abbey School, which he didn't enjoy. On leaving school, with few qualifications, he was unsure what to do. He tried for six months his vocation at Woodchester as a Dominican, an Order in which his brother Kenelm achieved great distinction as a scholar. It was not for him, but on leaving he experienced a strong urge to be a sculptor. There were no obvious influences governing this urge – as Kenelm later observed, it was akin to a vocation call – but he set about it with resolution.

He turned up at Eric Gill's workshop at Piggotts, near High Wycombe, one day in 1931 (leaving his suitcase in the hedge so as not to look too desperate!) and persuaded Gill to take him on as an apprentice. Within a few years he was Gill's main carver.

Gill was then at the height of his powers as a wood engraver, sculptor and typographer. His work ranged from the deeply religious to the erotic, reflecting the dichotomy of his private life in which his firm Catholicism somehow sat side by side with outrageous immorality. Anthony Foster shared his Faith but not his immorality.

Anthony had a deep love of the land and of nature and this, with his desire to see a fairer society, led him at Piggotts to embrace the Distributist Movement. The thinking behind this movement was advanced strongly in the 1930s by those two great writers and Catholic protagonists, G. K. Chesterton and Hilaire Belloc. Their political theory rejected both Capitalism and Socialism in favour of the creation of small farms and businesses run by the workers themselves. Gill too was a strong supporter. Anthony sought to implement the idea and was co-founder of the first Distributist community at Langenhoe in Essex.

In 1939 he married Wendy Heron, the sister of a Dominican friend, and they began their married life at another Distributist community at Laxton near Corby.

With the outbreak of war Anthony registered as a Conscientious Objector. When Laxton was taken to extend an airfield, he moved to Gill's farm at Piggotts, running the farm as his wartime service. After the war he returned to the workshop and to sculpture. Gill had died in 1940 but the family were trying to keep the business going. It was then that Anthony carved Gill's Crucifixion on the front of Guildford Cathedral.

In 1949 the Fosters moved to Frieth in Buckinghamshire where Anthony set up his own workshop. The last years of his life were dominated by ill-health. He managed to produce a lot of work in wood and stone. He rarely signed his work and kept almost no records of where his work went. Despite much physical pain, he managed also to feed his large family on home-grown vegetables and fruit, and home-reared chickens and geese.

He also taught two days a week at Camberwell School of Art. He was taken ill on his way there and died while being examined at St. Thomas's Hospital, leaving a wife and six children.

A humble man, as Foster was, who learnt his craft under such a large personality as Gill, will always be open to the suggestion that his work lacked originality, that it was too much like Gill's. Certainly his style was of the same genre but Kenelm's robust, but balanced, analysis in the *Blackfriars* magazine in 1953 identifies the distinguishing *"sober sweetness"* of Anthony's work, the greater expression in faces, a homely quality.

Anthony's six children inherited his artistic temperament and ability: Peter is a sculptor, Richard and Joseph are artists who also do some carving, Mary is an artist in Canada, Bernadette an artistic caterer and Christine is a connoisseur of art.

The Painting: *The Crucifixion* – Leonard Wyatt

Leonard Wyatt's *The Crucifixion* has hung above the main doors at St. Peter's since it was purchased by the then Vicar, the Revd. Lawrence Pickles, in 1959. With the Anthony Foster statue, it was dedicated at a Thanksgiving Service on 3rd July 1960 by the Bishop of Barking.

The painting was part of an exhibition in the tennis courts at Valentines Park in Central Ilford. The Revd. Pickles took members of the St. Peter's congregation to see the painting, including two youngsters who sang in the choir (the author and his late wife, in case you are wondering, but we were so young at the time and if the Vicar asked us to go to Valentines Park with him, we were most unlikely to refuse, having been brought up very properly to show respect for our betters!).

The crucifixion was an horrific event and the artist clearly intended to capture the starkness in his painting. From the moment it was first brought to St. Peter's people have either appreciated or disliked it – for the painting has been the subject of controversy over those 50 or so years (often vociferous and sometimes quite frightening to someone of a quiet disposition, such as the author of this book, who prefers in his dotage to keep his head down when the going is tough).

Leonard Wyatt (1922-2008) was born in Forest Gate and educated at Godwin Road Primary then Stratford Grammar School. Later he taught at Park Primary School in Newham. He began his training at the Hornsey College of Art when still a teenager, but then war broke out and he spent the next six years of his life in khaki, taking part in the D-Day landings in 1944.

After demob he had no difficulty in deciding his future course and resumed his studies at Hornsey, graduating in the early 1950s. He soon linked up with the Free Painters Group (FPG) in its very early days and remained an active member until poor health forced his retirement at the turn of the century.

His first one-man exhibition was at the Woodstock Gallery, London, in March 1960, and from that time he exhibited continuously in over 170 exhibitions – including 22 one-man shows. His paintings have been seen in most parts of the UK as well as in Norway, South Africa, USA and Germany. Two works have been purchased by the Museum of Modern Art in Allenstown, Pennsylvania. In 1987, he represented Britain with 11 large paintings in the 49th World Science Fiction Convention, held in Brighton, England. Although his themes frequently reflected man's quest into space, he was a lover of the English countryside, into which he frequently ventured; he also illustrated five rambling books.

Shortly after his death in 2008, after a long period suffering from Alzheimer's dementia, a retrospective exhibition of over 150 of Leonard's major works was held in his home town of Ilford.

Leonard's paintings are now being sold on a website. A provisional figure at auction for *The Crucifixion* was given in 2011 of £10,000.

The Sculpture: *The Woman of Samaria* – Thomas Bayliss Huxley-Jones

If you venture to the west end of the Churchyard at St. Peter's, where the Millennium Wall now stands, and look to the right (or the north if you happen to have a compass with you – as some folk do) you will find a piece of sculpture lurking amongst the bushes.

Like many works of art, people over the years have either loved it or disliked it – and at times there have been folk who would have taken matters into their own hands, going out at dead of night to hide the sculpture deep in the hedgerow and out of sight (or even removing it altogether!).

I hesitate to call such people vandals, but I doubt if they were art-lovers. But different folk have different tastes and we must not get over-excited about these things, especially when you are – like the author – living in your twilight years when every new day is a bonus to be enjoyed and savoured. From time to time the sculpture is covered with a green algae-like substance which kindly, diligent folk like Irene and Roger Kirby clean off. Good for them, I say, for we could do with a few more worthy souls who go about cleaning statues. It is fortunate that those who would have had the statue removed did not get their way.

Indeed they, and others, may be surprised to learn that the sculptor was an artist of some repute. For all we know the statue could be of some value – and that might make a few folk sit up and take note – as often happens when financial matters are in the offing!

The sculpture in fibreglass of *The Woman of Samaria* is registered thus at the Essex Record Office and bears the inscription: *'Springing up into eternal life'* (St. John, Chapter 4, vv 14) and the name Rose Jacobs (1882-1961). Originally Mr Jacobs, husband of Rose, had produced a plan for a proposed shelter over the seat in the Garden of Remembrance in her memory, but later expressed a preference for a piece of sculpture. The Parochial Church Council Minutes for 4th October 1961 record that following an approach to the Diocesan Advisory Board and a visit to Mr Huxley-Jones the sculptor, a statue was suggested. Members were shown a small model and were *"very happy to accept"* the gift with the proposal being agreed *"unanimously"*. The cost was £850 and a Service of Dedication was held in church on 23rd June 1962, conducted by the Revd. Pickles.

Aberdeen-born artist Thomas Bayliss Huxley-Jones, FRBS, ARCA (1908-1969). Huxley-Jones was a sculptor in a variety of materials who studied at Wolverhampton School of Art under Robert Emerson, 1924-29, and at the Royal College of Art, 1929-33, under Richard Garbe and Gilbert Ledward. He was married to the sculptor Gwyneth Holt. He exhibited at the Royal Academy (RA), The New England Arts Club (NEAC), The Royal Society to the encouragement of Arts, Manufactures and Commerce (RSA), The Society of Scottish Artists (SSA) and The Royal Birmingham Society of Artists (RBSA).

Huxley-Jones completed a large volume of public work: at the BBC Television Centre, London, in Chelmsford Cathedral, outside Hornsey Library and in London's Hyde Park. Aberdeen and Wolverhampton Art Galleries hold his work. Other works by Huxley-Jones include the fountain and gilded figure of Helios, the sun god of Greek mythology, located in the central courtyard of BBC Television Centre in London. Sea Fantasy in Aberdeen is a bronze sculpture of two dancing figures at the centre of a water pool.

He also cast a bronze sculpture of David Livingston, the African explorer, which stands in a niche on the Royal Geographical Society building, London. In 1953 Huxley-Jones won the Jean Masson Davidson Medal, the Society of Portrait Sculptors' highest award for distinguished services and outstanding achievement.

The Christ figure above the South Porch of St. Martin Le Tours Church, Basildon, is a fibreglass figure of Our Lord pierced by shafts of light, His hands outstretched towards the town in service of the people. It is an invitation of welcome to all to enter, designed and constructed by Huxley-Jones and erected in 1968. Just a few months after the statue had been officially dedicated, Huxley-Jones was admitted to St. John's Hospital, Chelmsford with a heart condition. He died there four days later on 10th December 1969, making this figure the last work he did.

The Stained Glass Windows at St. Peter's

When St. Peter's was consecrated in 1862, all but one of the windows were of plain glass – offering uninterrupted views across newly tilled farmland of Fairlop Plain towards Hainault Forest. Some of the stained glass is by Hardman and Co, founded in 1838 to become one of the world's leading manufacturers of stained glass and ecclesiastical fittings, and wound up in 2008. Buildings with stained glass by Hardman include Gloucester and Worcester Cathedrals, and the Houses of Parliament.

The East Window was the gift of Mr John Davis of Cranbrook Hall, Ilford, who chaired the Committee charged with raising sufficient sums to ensure the completion of the building of St. Peter's. This was the first stained glass window installed in St. Peter's and was probably in place at the time of the consecration. Three scrolls in stained glass at the top read: *"The Good Shepherd Giveth His Life For The Sheep"*. In the centre beneath is a representation of Jesus as the Good Shepherd *(far left)*, carrying a lamb and holding a shepherd's crook. This window was damaged during the Second World War and further deterioration required restorative work to be carried out in 1969 at a cost of £562. The coloured glass was replaced by an irregular pattern of green and opaque glass diamonds. Pieces of coloured glass may be seen in the top tracery – remnants of the original stained glass, perhaps?

The West Window was installed in 1875. It is a three-light window. The centre light depicts St. Peter *(above right)* carrying the crossed keys and a book, with a raised altar above his head. In the Gospel according to St. Matthew, Chapter 16, vv 19, Jesus said: *"And I will give unto thee the keys of the kingdom of heaven: and whatsoever thou shalt bind on earth shall be bound in heaven: and whatsoever thou shalt loose on earth shall be loosed in heaven."*

The crossed keys are to be found on the scarf of the 1st Aldborough Hatch (St. Peter's) Scout Group in memory of Mr Archie Titmarsh (known affectionately as 'Mr T') – Reader, Sunday School teacher and Group Scout Leader. A plaque in the church, the flagstaff on the Green and a seat outside the porch are all similar reminders of a man who influenced many lives in the post-war era of the 1940s to 1980s. Mr T is buried in the St. Peter's churchyard.

The remainder of the window is a simple pattern of coloured glass. The inscription is in two lines along the base and reads: *"To the Glory of God and in affectionate remembrance of George Painter of Aldborough Hall for many years Church Warden of this Parish, placed here Christmas 1875 by Friends and Neighbours."* The Painter family lived at Aldborough Hall from the 1850s until 1917.

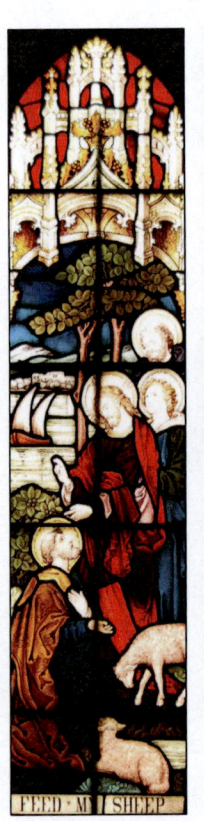

Another Painter family window is in the north wall of the Sanctuary depicting St. George *(far left)*. The dedication reads: *"In memory of George James Painter for many years Church Warden"*. The window on the opposite south wall of the Sanctuary shows St. Peter at the feet of Jesus *(left centre)* with the inscription *"Feed my sheep"* (St. John, Chapter 21, vv 16). The dedication reads: *"To the Glory of God in loving memory of my dear father and mother Charles Edward Lathbury, Vicar of this parish 1886-1901, and Frances Anne his wife who entered into rest May 8th 1897."* The window on the south wall of the Chancel depicts St. Mary and her Mother, St Anne *(above far right)*. The scroll reads: *"In loving memory of our dear father Charles James Painter."* On Sunday evening, 24th October 1916, the Right Revd. The Lord Bishop of Barking dedicated and unveiled this window.

The Painters of Aldborough Hall

The Painter family lived at Aldborough Hall from the 1850s until 1917 when the Hall stood at the junction of Aldborough Road North and Painters Road. Three Painters are buried in the Churchyard – Charles Alec Painter (11th February 1893 aged six months), John Henry Painter (22nd October 1902 aged 25) and Charles James Painter (18th March 1915 aged 77). A memorial plaque on the south side of the Chancel records that George Painter of Aldborough Hall was born on 21st January 1807 and died on 18th April 1875, aged 68, but he is not buried here. A memorial plaque on the north side of the Chancel records the two wives of George

Painter as follows: *"Sacred to the memory of Mary Harriett wife of George Painter of Aldborough Hall, Ilford, Essex who departed this life on l4th January 1852 aged 42 years and buried in Nunhead Cemetery. Also in affectionate remembrance of Harriett Susan, the second wife of the above, who departed this life on 23rd July 1873 aged 45 years likewise buried in Nunhead Cemetery. In life they were beloved and in death deeply lamented."*

The window on the South Wall in the body of the church, between the organ and the main door, depicts Faith and Dorcas *(left)*.

The scroll at the bottom reads: *"To the dear memory of Annie Kathleen Lake at rest 4th December 1931."* In the church records, Annie is noted as living at Aldborough House Farm and was aged 4l when she died.

The following was published in the St. Peter's Church Parish Magazine, February 1934: *"It is very gratifying that Archdeacon Bayne was able to come and dedicate the above. After a very gusty night and morning, the wind subsided, the weather improved and, as a result, the church was practically filled to its utmost capacity. The Service was intentionally short. but very impressive and the Archdeacon's address (if one may venture to say so) just fitted the occasion. Our church has a worthy memorial of Kathleen Lake, and has been greatly beautified by it. Once again, thanks to all who have made it possible. The artist's own description, appended herewith, may help to explain its deeper meaning;- 'The figures of Faith and Dorcas are chosen because they represent the life of Miss Lake – Faith and Works. The artist chose the 18th verse of the 2nd Chapter the Epistle of St. James for the sequence of the figures – 'Yea, a man may say, Thou hast faith and I have works: shew me thy faith without thy works, and I will shew thee my faith by my works.' In that verse the word 'Faith' precedes 'Works' no less than three times, so the figure is given preference by being placed on the left hand side. She is shown looking upward and holds with her right hand a cross, the emblem of our salvation. Dorcas 'a woman full of good works is shown holding a distaff with her right hand – an emblem of industry. On the small table at the side are various garments she has made for the poor. The background screens of flowers with birds in the foreground are associated with Miss Lake's life, which like the fragrance of the flowers and the sweet voices of the birds are gifts from God Himself. The Tracery openings above the long lights show the Phoenix – an emblem of the Resurrection, the Rose of Sharon and a Lilly – emblem of purity. In the lower portion of the long lights are the sacred monograms."*

The Lychgate at St. Peter's

The Lychgate (above) leading from the churchyard into Oaks Lane was the gift of the Revd. Pickles and his mother in 1961. Mrs Pickles died later that year and the dedication on the gates is in memory of both Revd. Pickles' father, Thomas Pickles (1871-1950) and his mother, Ada Florence (1877-1961). Renovation (left) was carried out in 2010. The shingles on the roof were replaced by Roger and Pam Goffee, and some timber was replaced. A Lychgate is a covered open structure at a church gate. The Saxon Lych means 'corpse' and gate meaning entrance – where a priest might conduct the first part of the funeral service.

The Artefacts at St. Peter's

Two antique chairs *(above left)* dated 1693 were presented to St. Peter's by Len and Joyce Chapman, who lived all their married life in Bawdsey Avenue, Aldborough Hatch, and were active members of St. Peter's over many years. The wooden panelling in the Sanctuary, the two Bishop's chairs *(above right)* and the brass processional cross were brought to St. Peter's from the Chapel of St. James, Little Heath, when this was demolished in 1933 *(see page 16)*.

The prayer desk *(above right)* is one of two in the Sanctuary, both made by Mr Dearlove who lived with his family in the bungalow opposite the Vicarage in Oaks Lane and who also made the two hymn boards. The prayer desks are dedicated to the memory of David Michael Greer, the son of Favell and David Greer, and the grandson of the Revd. Joseph Palanque Byng. Born in 1947, David died tragically in 1949 when he drowned in the lake in the Vicarage Garden *(see page 33)*.

At the Parochial Church Council Meeting on 25th January 1961, members voted 14 for and two against the gift by the Mothers' Union of the sounding board *(left)* over the pulpit. The Revd. Pickles spoke from the side of his mouth when preaching from the pulpit and gazed out of the nearby window. The sounding board helped those towards the rear of the church to hear what he was saying – for a sound system was not installed in the church until the 1990s.

The pulpit *(left)* was erected in memory of Churchwarden Isaac Lake, by friends and parishioners in 1919 at a cost of £95. The tiled floor is almost certainly the original flooring installed when the church was built. Similar tiles will be found near the main doors. The Chancel and Sanctuary were tiled in the same manner until the present floor was installed in the late 1950s. The rough stone area at the foot of the steps into the pulpit *(see above right)* is where the first pulpit was installed when the church was built – believed to be the raised stone platform on which the present pulpit stands, but in the corner reached by stone steps. Heating was by a stove at the North-West corner of the building, probably burning coal, coke and wood, with a chimney running up through the roof *(see photograph on page 38)*. Two cut planks may be seen where the chimney passed through the roof. In the accounts for the year Easter 1864 to Easter 1865, there is an item for £2.18s.0d for coals, two years later the sum fell to 13s. 9d.

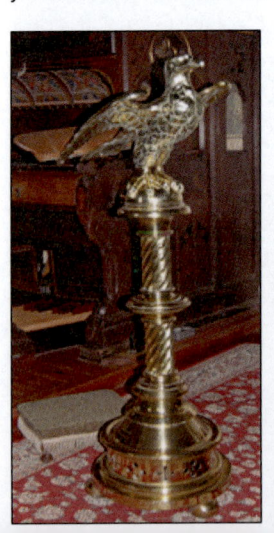

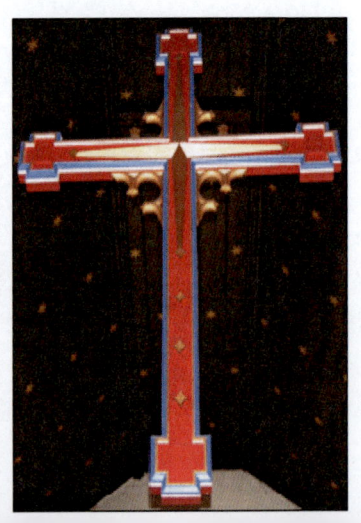

The Lectern *(far left)* was presented on Ascension Day 1914 by the wife of Captain William Griffiths, late of the 18th Royal Irish Regiment, who died on 24th January 1914 aged 72 years. Installed in 1950 in memory of Edward Gick and Ada Elizabeth Richardson, the Hanging Cross *(left)* was said by the Vicar to *"add beauty*

and dignity to our Church". The tops of the window arches were painted in colours matching the Hanging Cross following redecoration in 1983 by the Community Service Unit at the suggestion of the offenders who carried out the work of plastering and painting. At the same time as this work was being carried out, Lucy Allison and Doreen Mugford repainted the Hanging Cross, which was stored at Aldborough Hall Farm. The choir stalls were probably installed at the time of the consecration of the Church or soon after; the matching seat and desk where the Reader sits today were originally used by the Incumbent – the Vestry meeting for 1931 records that *"a handsome new seat and desk for the Vicar had been installed".*

The 1914-1918 War Memorial (left), erected in 1921/22, records the names of members of the Parish who gave their lives in the conflict. The inscription at the top of the painting reads: "To the Men of the Brave Sons of the Empire who fell on the battlefields of Europe. 'They have fought the good fight' dying in the cause of humanity that honour might live." The artist is unknown. At the Vestry Meeting in 1922, the Vicar thanked "Mr Fawcett for the trouble he had taken in the selection of a suitable design".

In 1964 at the time when the Vicarage was about to be sold to a builder *(see page 32)*, it is recorded that several friends of the Vicar, the Revd. Hesketh, were donating gifts to the Church in recognition of his Ministry. These included the Processional Cross and matching Candlesticks (all of which are wooden and in use in the church today); two decanters; a plated wafer box; prayer books and cottas for the crucifers. These were dedicated at Evensong on 20th December 1964. Perhaps a more poignant gift was that of a silver paten presented by the 1st Aldborough Hatch (St. Peter's) Scout Group in memory of Roger Frank, a young Scout who died from leukaemia, which was dedicated on 18th September 1966. It is inscribed: *"In Memorium Roger Frank 1947-1965 from his Brother Scouts".* Two carafes and a tray inscribed in memory of Yvonne are in use today.

The Jewish Grave at St. Peter's

Harry Walter Jassby in 1918

Born in Montreal, Harry Walter Jassby was a 19-year-old pharmacy student at McGill University, the son of Mr & Mrs Jassby of 4143 Oxford Avenue, Montreal, Canada. Wishing to fulfil his dream of becoming a pilot, he joined the Royal Flying Corps (forerunner of the Royal Air Force) in 1917 as Canada did not have an air force at the time. He lied about his age when he enlisted and his grave indicates he was 22 when, in fact, he was just 20. Before going overseas he learned to fly during his training as an aerial gunner in Canada near Toronto and was made a Second Lieutenant. Harry Jassby arrived in England in April 1918 where he was assigned to a squadron based at Fairlop Aerodrome. Second Lieutenant Jassby was learning how to fly the famous World War 1 fighter aircraft, the Sopwith Camel. The Biplane was extremely agile but also dangerous to fly, especially for service pilots. Jassby was among a group of men who had been asked to fly in a V-formation over London to celebrate the end of the war. Second Lieutenant Jassby was flying a Camel E142 when the plane above his lost its motor and collided with his, causing a crash. He died seven months after landing in England on 6th November 1918, just five days before Armistice Day. The practice at that time was to bury fallen servicemen in a cemetery nearest to their base and he was buried in the churchyard at St. Peter's. He received a Jewish burial service with military honours. Second Lieutenant Jassby was the last fatal wartime casualty of 54 Training Depot Squadron (TDS) at Fairlop Aerodrome.

By cruel co-incidence news of Second Lieutenant Jassby's death did not arrive until Armistice Day, 11th November. *"The Great War had ended and there was cheering and dancing in the streets of Montreal. The doorbell rang at my Grandmother's home. A telegram was delivered,"* Carolyn Steinman, his niece, said. *"My mother opened it and read the dreadful news to her mother Minerva."* It was a dreadful blow. Minerva's husband, Louis Jassby, had died in 1914 at the age of 39 leaving her a widow with seven children. *"Uncle Harry loved to fly,"* said Carolyn, whose mother, the late Lottie Notkin, was Jassby's sister and the last of his six siblings to survive. She died in 1994 aged 93. When this was researched in 2004, in addition to Carolyn, Second Lieutenant Jassby was survived by his nephews Kenny (in Israel), Danny and Alan (in the United States) and Carolyn's sister, Lois Spiegel, and brother Harry Notkin, his namesake, as well as many great nieces and nephews.

In January 1985 Carolyn and her husband, Arnold, visited the grave at St. Peter's for the first time after making enquiries with the Commonwealth War Graves Commission. They met the Rabbi of the Southwest Essex Reform and Reform Synagogue, Oaks Lane, and the Vicar of St Peter's. The Rabbi and Carolyn's husband recited Kaddish and the Vicar said a prayer. *"This was an extremely emotional moment in my life,"* said Carolyn. *"I mentioned that maybe his body could be removed to a Jewish Cemetery, but both clergy were quite adamant that his resting place should remain as it is."* The War Graves Commission wrote to Carolyn explaining that its principle throughout the world is that the graves of the war dead, whether they died in battle or by other cause, *"should not be disturbed unless there is some overriding reason in the public interest"* such as the construction of a road that could not be alternatively routed.

Second Lieutenant Jassby's grave is on the left inside the front gate at St. Peter's. The Star of David together with the insignia of the Royal Air Force appears on his tombstone with the inscription: *'In life he flew the azure sky, in death he flew to heaven high.'* The grave is maintained by members of the local Jewish community, who visit it regularly and follow the tradition of placing a pebble or stone on the top of the gravestone to signify that someone has honoured the deceased person's memory with a visit. Those of us who have been privileged to witness the gathering have been struck by the dignity of the participants and the solemnity of the occasion.

The Churchyard at St. Peter's

This is a 'Spot the Difference' contest with no prizes. The top shot, circa 1941, is taken from just inside what would become the 'New' Churchyard – prior to that it was part of the Vicarage Meadow – and you can see the tufted grass of a meadow at the bottom left. The photograph (above) was taken on 20th September 2011 with the two gravestone crosses lined up on either side of the window to the left of the porch as in the top shot. Note that there is no sapling sycamore in the top shot that is now a huge tree in the second photograph. Now look at the photograph on the next page . . .
(I trust you are still with me, but if not please persevere!).

In the photograph *(above)*, taken on 20th September 2011, the full height of the hedge separating the 'Old' from the 'New' Churchyard may be seen in all its glory – with a very fine Paladin and two good quality dustbins standing side by side in true military fashion (bought from B & Q or, more probably, Homebase). Look very closely and you will see those two gravestone crosses peeping over the top of the hedge (and you will appreciate now why I asked you to persevere). The old Churchyard was consecrated on 15th October 1875 (the first person buried was Johnathan Miller of Marks Gate, Little Heath, aged 78, on 17th February 1876, with E. Norton Eldrid presiding), but why am I so sure when the 'New' Churchyard was first opened up to the burial of the dead? Well, the list of graves compiled on a Microsoft Works Database by Reader Brian Kerrison in the first decade of the 21st Century (and probably with some help from the late and much lamented Una Paul) shows quite clearly and conclusively that the first grave in Area C (which is in the 'New' Churchyard) is that of none other than Charles Thomas Goodall of Morton Road, Seven Kings, who died aged 77 years on 19th December 1941 and was buried on 23rd December in the first row of Area C, with the Revd. Joseph Palanque Byng presiding. Next came Millie Selina Compton of Meads Lane, who departed this life in the midst of World War II on 20th December 1941 aged 57 years and was buried on the day after Boxing Day (also St. Stephen's Day, it should be noted) on 27th December. There followed a few days grace for the Revd. Byng to enjoy the rest of the festive season and to see the New Year in, until 23rd January when he buried Bert Frederick Nicoll of Crownfield Avenue, a young man of only 20, who died on 16th January. It is interesting (well, I think so!) that there is an entry here for Ellen Partridge whose ashes were interred on 27th May 1941 – perhaps one of the first such to be cremated and interred here.

There are many interesting – and often intriguing – gravestones in the Churchyard at St. Peter's. The above is just one such for it is the grave of William George Eglin, who was known affectionately to his family and friends as Billie. He, poor soul, was killed by a City Bus in Ilford on the 4th of June 1936 at the tender age of 39. He was, the stone assures us, a *'Devoted Husband and loving Daddy'* – which is good to know. This gravestone was pointed out to me by Jeanette Pointing on 20th September 2011 – who told me that Billie was a great friend of her father which, again, is good to know. And here *(above)* is a City Bus, of the kind that killed poor Billie Eglin. The City Omnibus Co Ltd was registered in 1923 and was a 'pirate' operator within the Capital. But with the formation of the London Passenger Transport Board in 1923 the days of City's operations were numbered. In an attempt to preserve its name, the City Company in 1928 bought a controlling interest in New Empress Saloons which had pioneered a route (No. 256) from Wood Green to Southend via Gants Hill, Ilford and Romford Market. The City fleet of 39 vehicles was transferred to New Empress but retained the oval 'City' operating logo and the brown and cream colours. I rode a City Bus to Southend – it was a bone-shaker with hard seats!

(Above) The 'New' Churchyard shot on Friday 14th May 2010 – again from the roof of the church halls. To mark the Millennium, a Memorial Wall (left) was built in the south west corner of the Churchyard.

Dedicated by the Bishop of Barking in January 2000, the Wall is 9 metres in length and 1.25 metres high, and is in the form of a right angle with splayed corner incorporating a memorial panel. Constructed in selected brick with stone capping and waist course, recessed panels will accommodate 400 black-finished cast-bronze individual memorial plaques. A stone paved area surrounds the wall with limited facilities for cut flowers. The Garden of Remembrance Memorial Wall is a memorial for those whose ashes are interred in the Garden of Remembrance. St.

Peter's raised £8,424 locally through generous donations, a Gift Day, concerts (featuring the New Redbridge Wind Orchestra, Ted Heath and Friends, and Claire London), and an Auction of Gifts and Promises. We received a welcome grant from London-over-the-Border, a diocesan-based charitable funding body, and a grant of £5,000 from Lafarge Redland through the Landfill Tax Credit Scheme. The Scheme reallocates tax levied on the landfill operator, who in turn is able to sponsor projects near the site. Lafarge Redland was involved – and continues to be – in the latter part of the last century and the early part of the 21st Century in sand and gravel extraction on Fairlop Plain within the parish of St. Peter.

(Above) The Garden of Remembrance, opened in 1958, in the 'New' Churchyard looking east with the Lychgate leading into Oaks Lane. (Left) Roger and Irene Kirby at work on the flower beds in the Garden of Remembrance in the Spring of 2011.

'Planted to commemorate the Coronation of H M Queen Elizabeth II 1953' is the inscription on a small grey metal plaque in the centre of three rose beds in the Churchyard, in front of the porch *(above)*. Some new roses have been planted over the years, but others are thought to be originals. The Californian Poppies *(Eschscholzia Californica)* self-seeded in the early years of the 21st Century. Self-seeding occurs all over the Hatch, but the lady who vowed in 2010 that the Téte a Téte narcissus in the Shrubberies in Aldborough Road North were self-seeded by the birds had it wrong – but would not be persuaded that they were planted as bulbs by a locally renowned 'Guerrilla Gardener' (who will be nameless).

Roses in bloom in September 2011. The garden is lovingly tended by folk at St. Peter's who are often seen deadheading in the summer.

(Top) Over the Rose Garden to the church halls from inside the church porch and (above) the view from Aldborough Road North – both shot in the Spring of 2011.

St. Peter's Flower Festivals

St. Peter's Flower Festival is held over the weekend nearest to St. Peter's Day – 29th June – our Patronal Festival.

The Flower Festival started in a small way in 1981. For as long as many can remember – and some of us are so old (and that includes me, as you ask!) that we can remember things that happened years and years and years ago, and even before that – St. Peter's held a Garden Party on a Saturday afternoon in high summer, always in bright sunshine, in the old Vicarage Garden, at Aldborough Hall Farm, Aldborough House Farm or in the Church Hall grounds on the Green. In 1981 it was decided to stage a Flower Festival in Church to run alongside the Saturday afternoon Garden Party in the Church Hall grounds. Flowers were arranged on Friday evening and Saturday morning, and taken down that evening. From those small beginnings the Festival has grown to a three-day event. On Saturday and Sunday there is a Craft Market in the Church Halls, displays by local organisations on the Green, and Services and Choral Recitals in Church. The Church is open on Monday for visitors and for children from local schools. It is said that hundreds, even thousands, attend the event nowadays so popular is it.

'People who made a difference' was the Flower Festival theme in 2007 when the first display in the Churchyard depicted George Stephenson's *'Rocket'*.

The following are the themes of the Festivals over three decades or so:

1981:	Benedicite, omnia opera *(0 all ye works of the Lord, bless ye the Lord)*	1997:	Stories from the Bible
		1998:	Thank you, Lord
		1999:	AD 1999 – Towards the Millennium
1982:	Festivals of the Church in flowers	2000:	Children's Classic Stories
1983:	Life in Aldborough Hatch – the village in the suburbs	2001:	Musicals
		2002:	The Queen's Golden Jubilee
1984:	The Parables of our Lord	2003:	The Writings of Charles Dickens
1985:	The Saints	2004:	A treasury of poetry
1986:	Stories from the Old Testament	2005:	Let's Celebrate – Twenty-five years of St. Peter's Flower
1987:	Songs of Praise		
1988:	Celebration Flower Festival – 125 Years of St. Peter's	2006:	Art in Flowers
		2007:	People who made a difference
1989:	The Life of St. Peter	2008:	Sing Glory
1990:	The Sanctity of Marriage	2009:	Our green and pleasant land
1991:	St. Peter the Apostle	2010:	Pearls of Wisdom
1992:	The Glory of the Garden	2011:	Rhymes from the Nursery
1993:	The Life of Christ	2012:	The Best of Britain
1994:	All things bright and beautiful	2013	Underground Overground
1995:	God's gifts	2014	Let's go to the Movies
1996:	Let all the world in every corner sing	2015	Two of a Kind
		2016	Brush up your Shakespeare

The St. Peter's Morris Team made their debut at the 1988 Festival, where they were a regular feature until 2005, when some found leaping with sticks too much! Later ladies joined, but here (left) are the first Morris Men. Photographed 1988 in their original costumes – with variegated neckerchiefs rather than the red and blue ones favoured in later years – they are (from left to right) Martyn Stewart, Patrick Fitzgibbons, Ron Jeffries, Roger Menear, Derek Smith, Richard May and Brian Kerrison. These Morris Men were following in the footsteps of Will Kemp, a morrice (note the spelling!) dancer who in 1599 made a bet that he would dance along the road from London to Norwich – which he did, jingling his bells, in nine days dancing with 18 days of rest! His diary records that he "stopped at Ilford . . . being offered carouses in the great spoon, one whole draught being able at that time to have drawne my little wit drye". Today the Great Spoon of Ilford (a vessel made of pewter with a long handle holding more than a quart of ale) is commemorated in Ilford Town Centre with a public house of that name.

The Redbridge Asian Mandal performing at the 2011 Flower Festival.

Music students from Oaks Park High School perform on the Green during the 30th Anniversary Flower Festival in 2010 – one of a number of local organisations taking part in the entertainment during the weekend

Loraine Porter and Vicki Palmer with members of the Palmerstone Dancers – who have appeared at every Festival since 1991 (see also page 109).

Aldborough Hall and Equestrian Centre

Aldborough Hall was built in the 1830s at the north-west corner of what is today the junction of Aldborough Road North and Painters Road. In the 1850s the Hall was owned by the Painter family until the early years of the 20th Century when a member of the McAdam family – famous for its macadam road building technology – took over the Hall. During World War II the Hall was used as an Officers' Mess by the nearby Fairlop Airfield. The building fell into disrepair after the war until Bob and Mary Garrett undertook major renovation and rebuilding. A cottage, hayloft and stables were saved and incorporated into the new buildings of the Aldborough Hall Equestrian Centre – founded by Bob in 1956 and which Mary continues to run as proprietor following Bob's sad death in 2016.

Charles Painter sits outside the front door of a one-down, one-up cottage at Aldborough Hall with members of his staff in 1902.

Bob and Mary Garrett (front row) with (from left to right) their daughter Sarah, son Robert, and Lynette Harding, Mary's sister, re-enacting the photograph of 1902 – outside the same cottage in 1980, by which time this was being used by the Equestrian Centre as the Tack Room.

The Conservatory at Aldborough Hall – the main Hall was immediately behind. The Aldborough Tree, planted in the 1830s, is seen on the right and (below centre) as it is today – with both the tree (now 180 or so years old) and the lawn very much as it was all those years ago.

When Bob applied to the then Ilford Council for planning permission to build their flat, a lady Councillor expressed concern on learning that the flat would be on the first floor and approached by an outside stone staircase. "How," she asked, all wide-eyed, "how will you get the horses up those stairs?"

The main buildings and stables at Aldborough Hall Equestrian Centre, photographed on Friday 16th September 2011.

The Dick Turpin –
From Beer House to Public House to Restaurant

The original Dick Turpin was a beer house in one of the Aldborough Hall Farm Cottages to the north of the present building. These cottages are believed to date back to the 16th Century. The 1861 Census lists James Cole (73, born at Weald, Essex) as Beer House Keeper, his wife Martha (61), and sons George (41) and Thomas (31), both dealers – wife and sons were born in Barking. Both sons are buried in St. Peter's Churchyard – George in 1888 and Thomas in 1901. Thomas took over as Beer House Keeper in 1881 and Emily Cole, niece of Thomas, from 1902 to 1914. From 1917 Ernest Perkins is listed as Beer Retailer – it is believed that Ernest is seated on the right of the photograph above. The signs above the doors read Public Bar and Bar Parlour. The cottages burned down in a fire in September 1966.

This photograph is dated c1912 – at around the time the new Dick Turpin opened its doors. Aldborough Hall Farm cottages – site of the beer house – are seen on the left. In both photographs the brewers are shown – Mann, Crossman and Paulin.

The following account of the V2 Rocket which dropped outside the Dick Turpin in November 1944 is by Keith Tranmer, a long-time resident of Aldborough Hatch:

"I was a part-time air raid warden at post No. 22 or 25 (I have forgotten the number) located in the banjo of Bawdsey Avenue. Like most others, our duties were confined to night shifts after work, usually one night a week. We slept in the dugout and answered the telephone, but during raids the dugout was filled with the other wardens. There were full-time staff during the day. There was an air raid in progress on the Saturday morning (approximately 9am to 10am) of the day of the incident. I responded from home going straight to the scene. I was a bit delayed because I was in the bath at the time. It was a V2 rocket which had impacted on the forecourt of the Dick Turpin public house. On the way to the scene I saw Mrs Dipper, who lived at 6 Applegarth Drive and was a cleaner at the Dick Turpin. She was in a distressed state, her face and arms cut from flying glass. She was the first war widow in our locality in 1939 when her husband, a regular sailor in the Royal Navy, went down with the 'Royal Oak' in Scapa Flow. I stopped to help her, but she wanted to get home to her daughter who was left on her own. When I arrived at the scene I saw the crater and nearby three bodies – two of them were RAF Officers and the third was the landlord at the Dick Turpin, Phil Perkins. A badly damaged RAF staff car was nearby. The whole of the area, the bodies and the staff car, were showered with cigarettes, suggesting that an exchange was going on when the rocket landed – drinks for cigarettes? The RAF Officers came from their quarters at Aldborough Hall, where the Aldborough Hall Equestrian Centre is sited today. The National Fire Service and the Police were already on the scene. Some were in the building and down the cellar - from where a fireman emerged with a large vase full of banknotes. I left shortly afterwards as there was nothing I could do."

Phil Perkins (43) was killed when the V2 struck. One of his forbears, Rifleman Albert Edward Perkins, fell in France in 1917 and he is commemorated in the church and on the family grave in the churchyard. Also killed was Leading Aircraftman W. G. Skeet (40) who was cycling by when he stopped to talk with Phil when the missile struck. He is interred in the war graves section at Barkingside Old Cemetery, Longwood Gardens.

There is no record of Dick Turpin riding through Aldborough Hatch – although he might have done so on his way to and from Barking. Dick Turpin was baptised in 1705 at Hempstead in Essex where his father, John, was landlord of the Blue Bell Inn (later the Rose and Crown). Dick became a butcher and married Elizabeth (Betty) Millington. From about 1730 the couple lived at Buckhurst Hill and Turpin became involved with a gang of deer-stealers led by a blacksmith named Samuel Gregory. The gang turned to housebreaking, terrorising isolated farms and houses on the fringes of London. *The London Gazette*, 22nd to 25th February 1734, offered a reward of fifty pounds (a lot of money) for information leading to the arrest of one Richard Turpin *("very much mark'd with the Small Pox . . . wears a Blew Grey Coat and a light natural Wig . . . charged upon Oath for committing several*

Robberies in Essex"). On 19 December 1734 Dick Turpin and friends robbed the Skinner family of Longbridge Farm, Barking, of items valued at some £300, *"tossing money to crowds of bystanders"* as they escaped through Barking – all part of Dick's robbing the rich to give to the poor, no doubt. On 7 April, 1739, Dick Turpin was executed in York for horse-stealing.

The Dick Turpin pub sign on Aldborough Road North where it had stood for many years, photographed in the 1980s, depicting the man himself riding Black Bess on one of his notorious rampages – but not, as far as we know, in Aldborough Hatch.

The bar at the rear of the Dick Turpin in 1961 – John Roper (far left) with friends Gerald Risby and Terry Wood, all of whom spent their childhood in Applegarth Drive, Aldborough Hatch, and were active members of the Church and Scout Group. Note the figure of Dick Turpin on Black Bess, his horse, on the window.

Miller & Carter – not the Dick Turpin – in 2010, but the story does not end there.

78

Long, long ago – in fact, as long ago as 2006 – I made contact with Miller & Carter, part of Mitchells & Butler, to ask why they had dropped the name 'Dick Turpin' from our local hostelry. I met a top man from M & C who told me that there was no way that they would ever countenance a return to the 'Dick Turpin'. *"No, not never,"* he said, with a stern look on his face. He went further and said that they did not wish to be a pub with a restaurant attached, but a classy steak house. They introduced rules of dress. No jeans. No farm labourers (of whom we had a dwindling few). No muddy boots. No children. But things did not go well for M & C as folk started to stay away. And so they relaxed the dress rules a little – but still no farm labourers or muddy boots, and certainly no children. Then there were financial troubles and the PR man who had sent me so many emails about upper crust dining and brand names departed faster than I can walk from my home to the 'Dick Turpin'. But we locals – and folk from afar – kept calling it the 'Dick Turpin'. It was listed in the telephone directory as the 'Dick Turpin'. If you rang to book a table they said *"Dick Turpin"*. And your credit card slip said 'Dick Turpin'.

Early in 2011 the time was right to have another go, for the financial problems seemed to be a thing of the past. The former PR man had produced a sketch and I sent this off to M & C. A pleasant executive called Oliver told me that they would never put the words 'Dick Turpin' back on a sign. Emails went back and forth – and even forth and back. *"No, no,"* said Oliver. *"Yes, yes,"* said I. Then I brought out the *Big Guns*. The story appeared on the Barkingside 21 website (and you do not get a Bigger Gun than that) and Oliver promised to reconsider, as I hinted that I might involve the *Ilford Recorder* (an even Bigger Gun, if that were possible). On Wednesday 21st September 2011, two men erected a board below the M & C sign proudly declaring that 'Dick Turpin' rode again *(see photograph at top of page)*. A spokesman for M & C told the *Ilford Recorder*: "We are fully aware that many local people know and love the business as the Dick Turpin and we are more than happy to incorporate the historic name with the M & C name." And I quietly rejoiced that, after five years of fighting I had not only won the battle but the war, too, for that does not happen often in this life! And there was great rejoicing, both locally and afar, that the name Dick Turpin was on display again.

Cuckoo Hall

An 18th Century house in a walled garden stood on the east side of Aldborough Road North, occupied in 1777 by a Captain Williams. This was probably the Old Clock House, demolished in the early 19th Century except for the red-brick garden walls with gabled coping and a former gazebo with a hip tiled roof.

(Top left) This photograph, dated circa 1950, was scanned from a booklet published by the Dick Turpin at around that time. (Top right) The same elevation in 2010. (Above left) The rear of the gazebo and wall after ivy had been cleared – August 2011. (Above right) The roof seen from inside the building – August 2011. The first floor had disappeared, the window openings changed and the doorways boarded up. A more correct name for Cuckoo Hall is said to be 'Cook Koo Hall'.

Today the gazebo and wall stand within the grounds of the Dick Turpin – leased to Miller & Carter by the London Borough of Redbridge. Both the gazebo and the wall are Locally Listed. Following representations in 2011, Miller & Carter and the Borough agreed to carry out essential repairs to maintain the building for any possible future use, see page 115 for the latest position.

St. Chad's Well

*(Above left) St. Chad's Well in 1902.
(Top right) The site of St. Chad's Well in 2011 in Billet Road looking west, marked by a brick-built plinth surmounted by a tablet (right) reading: 'St. Chad's Well – The site of St. Chad's Well from which the name Chadwell Heath is derived. This tablet was placed here by the Ilford Borough Council on behalf of the Citizens of Ilford to commemorate the Festival of Britain 1951'.*

George Tasker records: *"Possibly a small settlement existed* (at Chadwell Heath) *as far back as the days of the early Saxons, viz., at the time when Cedde or Ceadda was Bishop of London . . . Cedde had a brother named Chad, who was also a pious man and a great missionary . . . at his death in 672-3 . . . was Bishop of the Mercians".* Writing in 1901, Tasker reports that there was a reputed medicinal well in Billet Lane *"which was at one time resorted to by persons with weak eyesight for the special properties of the water . . . It is said that Cedde held a baptism at this spot, and because of the healing qualities of the water, and in memory of his brother Chad, whose fame had spread all over the country, it became known as St. Chad's Well . . . The water is of excellent quality; it has never been known to fail, and there is a constant running off of the surplus . . ."* Today, the *'alcove of brickwork' (top left)* recorded by Tasker has disappeared.

In 1951 I carried the Brass Processional Cross at the head of the Choir – from St. Peter's via Applegarth Drive and the A12 – to Billet Road, where choir and people sang hymns with gusto (well, those with puff left did so) and the Bishop of Chelmsford and the Revd. Lawrence Pickles mounted a flatbed vehicle to conduct a short service of dedication. We passed the site of the Chapel of St. James at the junction of the A12 and Barley Lane from whence the Cross came to St. Peter's when the Chapel was demolished in 1933 *(see pages 16 to 18)*.

The Farms and Farmhouses of Aldborough Hatch

The farms across Fairlop Plain date back some 160 years or so to 1851 when the area was disafforested (referred to earlier) and the large farmhouses were built. The farms within the parish of Aldborough Hatch were Aldborough Hall Farm, Aldborough Hatch Farm, Aldborough House Farm, Whites Farm and Hainault Farm – with others on the periphery. The first three were on Crown land and leased from Michaelmas to Michaelmas and were farmed jointly until 13th October 1956, when Charles Peter Rudge and his sons, Peter and Charles (Bob) Rudge, took over Aldborough Hall Farm and Dick Lewis moved into the farmhouse of Aldborough House Farm and farmed both Aldborough House and Aldborough Hatch Farms. Married in 1957, Peter and Shirley Rudge moved into Aldborough Hall Farm, where their three daughters Ann, Jenny and Sally were born. Tragedy struck in November 1962 when Bob Rudge was drowned when his tractor overturned on the farm in Seven Kings Water. Sadly, Charles Peter Rudge died in 1977 and his son, Peter, in December 2005. Shirley now owns the farmhouse and adjacent buildings and land. Two barns at Aldborough Hatch Farm are Locally Listed. The large timber barn is probably 18th Century. It is weather boarded with corrugated asbestos cement roof, with an outbuilding with pantile roof to the east. Some of the original timbers include undressed branches forming natural joints. The second barn, circa 1850, is a typically built machine sawn softwood building.

(Above) Aldborough Hall Farm and the Dick Turpin seen from Lake Cottages.

Aldborough House Farm

Aldborough House Farm *(left)* was built on Oaks Lane in 1856. The first reference to a Mr Lake at a St. Peter's Vestry Meeting is in 1867. Isaac Lake was Church-warden from 1879 to 1886 – and died in 1918 – so we can surmise that the Lake Family farmed from here from the 1860s. We have it on good authority that in the 1920s and early 1930s, the farm 'belonged' to Rupert Brown, but was run by Clement Lake who lived in the farmhouse with his mother, Ann, and his sister, Annie Kathleen. All three are buried in St. Peter's Churchyard – Annie Kathleen died in 1931 aged 41 (and has a memorial window in the church – see page 57), Clement died in 1934 aged 46 and Ann died in 1936 aged 83. Arthur Edwards was the next occupant of Aldborough House Farm. He lived there with his sister as a bachelor until he married in the early 1950s. His new wife, Audrey, was much younger and something of a blonde bombshell, much admired by my fellow choir members and me, as she sat in the front pew below the pulpit and fairly ogled the Vicar, the Revd. Pickles. There were rumours at the time that Audrey did not hit it off with Farmer Edwards' sister and that she had gone through his money in the one year or so that they were married – and he shot himself in the cellar at the Farm on the first anniversary of his wedding, where farmhand John Lindsell found him. There is an anecdotal story of this time. Laurence Stringer JP was a member of the well-known and highly respected Ilford Stringer family. A magistrate and Group Scout Leader of the 5th Seven Kings Scout Group, Laurence later held national appointments in The Scout Association, leading the Windsor Parade of Queen's Scouts over many years and being awarded the CBE. At the time of Farmer Edwards' death, Laurence ran the family wholesale potato business in Spitalfields Market, rising at 4am each day to be in the market early. On the night of Farmer Edward's death, Laurence arrived late at a Group Scouters' Meeting at the 5th Seven Kings, where he announced in his stentorian voice: *"I have had a dreadful day. The price of potatoes went up, there were traffic jams all the way from London and my Uncle has shot himself. We will commence the meeting in*

prayer." Richard Quennell Lewis – Dick, Dickie or Rustle to his many friends (the latter because he wore a weatherproof coat that rustled) – took on the farm in 1956. Dick and his wife, Mary were stalwarts of St. Peter's, with their daughters, Amanda and Elizabeth. Mary died in 1980 and Dick in 1993. Elizabeth and her husband, Andrew Abbott, purchased the buildings of Aldborough House Farm and live there to this day with their son, Phillip.

(Above left) The summerhouse in the garden of Aldborough House Farm c1930 with Dolly and Kathleen Lake and (above right) in 2011. The summerhouse, on rails which turn to catch the sun, was built for one of the Lake daughters who had tuberculosis and died there. Amanda recalls that she and her sister would "spin it as fast as we could – our own roundabout!" (Below) The house in 2011.

(Above left) Clement Lake and (right) barns at Aldborough House Farm c1930.

(Above left) Aldborough House Farm c1930 – much as it is today but without the pond.
(Above right) John Lindsell – in yellow jacket – harvesting vegetable crops for the London markets in the 1960s. John lived in one of the cottages in Painters Road. (Left) Horse-drawn machinery on Aldborough House Farm in the 1930s.

85

Aldborough Hatch Farm

Built two years earlier in 1854, Aldborough Hatch Farm was amalgamated with Aldborough House Farm when farmland was lost with the building of the Oaks Lane Estate in the late 1940s. When Dick Lewis took over both farms in 1956, the house had been condemned and was to be demolished, but Dick used it for storing potatoes in the kitchen! The top flat was done up and inhabited by various couples just married needing a cheap flat – one of these was Graham and Margaret Austin. Amanda married Peter Schlotter, moving into the house and swopping their cottage with Lynn Morris in May 1979, with the task of turning it back into a house. In the kitchen there were iron bars at the windows and across the back door. Amanda and Peter moved to the Essex coast in 2006.

Aldborough Hatch Farm photographed in the 1980s or 1990s. The dog is Bertie.

*(Above) Dick Lewis at Aldborough Hatch Farm, 25th June 1992.
(Left) Peter Schlotter, Gary Millhouse, Dick Lewis, Tubby Sammons, John Elsip, with (in front) Matthew Schlotter and Bertie the dog in the 1990s
(Below) Aldborough Hatch Farm Autumn 2011.*

Aldborough Hall Farm

Aldborough Hall Farm was probably built around 1855 and was run by the Rudge family from 1956 as tenant farmers. In 1957 Peter Rudge married Shirley and their daughters Ann, Jenny and Sally lived with them at the farm. Corn, potatoes and vegetables were grown later expanding into 'Pick Your Own' fruit and vegetables. The farm shop opened in the mid-60s. The farm worked closely with the RSPCA to rescue animals for the public to see including pigs, sheep, donkeys, goats, rabbits and birds. In 2004 Redbridge Council reclaimed the farmland for gravel extraction and the 'Pick Your Own' had to cease. The farm shop closed in late 2006, the animals and most of the birds were rehomed and the farm closed to the public.

(Left) The yard at Aldborough Hall Farm. The brick wall – which runs at the rear of the Farm and behind the Dick Turpin and Cuckoo Hall – is 18th Century and Locally Listed. The willow tree behind the pond blew down in a gale in 2015 and has been replaced.

The Smithy

The Smithy blacksmith's forge *(above)* of T. E. Smith and Son, was situated on Aldborough Hall Farm at the south-east corner of the junction of Painters Road with Aldborough Road North. A smithy is shown there from 1881. Kelly's *Directory of Essex* 1894 lists T. H. Smith under smiths, blacksmiths and farriers in Aldborough Hatch. The 1901 Census lists The Shoeing Forge with Thomas H. Smith (Wheelwright) in occupation with wife, two daughters and son, Frederick (Blacksmith). Kelly's Directory of Essex 1902 has an entry for Thomas Henry Smith, Blacksmith, in Aldborough Hatch. In the photograph *(above)* c1904, the trade of Van and Cart Builders is shown below the name.

The Saunders family probably moved from Great Ellingham, Norfolk, to Aldborough Hatch between 1907 and 1910. At the 1911 Census, John and Jane Saunders are listed with their son, Walter (21), and daughter, Edie (16), together with three sons at school (George [12], Baden [10] and Port [7]) and a daughter and son at home (Ivy [4] and William [1]). John's occupation is shown as blacksmith and son Walter's as farrier. All the children were born in Norfolk with the exception of William who was born in Aldborough Hatch. The three sons at school probably attended the Aldborough Hatch Church of England School next door to St. Peter's, which closed in 1912 *(see page 44)*. The 1911 Census shows the forge as uninhabited and the Forge Cottages occupied by the Saunders family. Thomas Smith had retired and in 1911 was living at the White House, Kelvendon Common, Brentwood.

The Smithy is marked on the OS Maps dated 1905 and 1914 *(see pages 9 and 10)* and was probably demolished in the early years of the 20th Century.

Willow Farm

The house at Willow Farm *(above)* in Billet Road was built in the late 1800s – the oldest part being at the rear *(left)*. Little is known of the first occupants. In the mid-1920s, Chadwell Heath farm labourer Charles Peter Rudge married Catherine Foster of Padnal Corner. With a family on the way, Charles needed a better paid job, so he left the land and became a hod-carrier on the house-building sites in Goodmayes. The depression struck and Charles lost his job, but when the tenancy for Willow Farm came up, he took the bold step of taking it, moving into the farmhouse in 1927 with their young family and farming the land which stretched south over what is now the A12 and down Barley Lane. Their eldest daughter, Lydia, died aged 14 in 1935 when a motorist hit her as she cycled to work at the junction of Billet Road and Hainault Road. Daughter Hilda died in 1927 aged three, whilst Charles William (always known as Bob) died in a tractor accident and Peter died in 2005 *(see page 82)*. Sister Doris celebrated her 80th birthday in 2011. Catherine died in 1973 and Charles Peter in 1977 – both are buried at St. Peter's. Willow Farm stood empty from 1977 until Clive Wilderspin moved there in 1978 – with the ghosts and a dog. Ann Rudge and Clive were engaged that year and married in September 1979. They live there with son Martin whilst daughter Sarah is living in Portsmouth.

Whites Farm

Whites Farm on Oaks Lane was associated with the family of John Le White (1285) but otherwise the earliest reference to the estate was in 1540. The farm persisted as an independent unit with the same boundaries from the Middle Ages until early in the 20th Century. It is recorded that John Fountain farmed here and sold peas and other produce at the market abutting Southwark Cathedral in 1901 (the site of Borough Market today). The farmhouse (*above*) dates from 1860, distinguished with an ironwork verandah. Today the East London Christian Fellowship Centre (ELCFC) is based here – an evangelical Christian church whose services are conducted in English and Chinese (Cantonese and Mandarin). There is said to be some evidence for medieval (1066 -1539 AD) and early post-medieval activity in the area including the survival of Oaks Lane and nearby Chase Lane, both of which have medieval origins, which must make them the oldest thoroughfares in Aldborough Hatch. Approximately 0.5km north-west of the site on Chase Lane stood two late medieval or early post medieval mills – a watermill (circa 1616) fed by three ponds and a windmill (circa 1666-1685). By 1725 the buildings had gone but the area was known as Mill Ground.

Oaks Park High School (founded 2001) stands to the south of Whites Farm with its playing fields to the north – the latter on land that was an open sand and gravel pit in the 1930s. I know this to be a fact, because I fell into the water when fishing with my elder brother! Post-war the pits were in-filled with household rubbish and a variety of derelict vehicles before a recreation ground was created – part of which remains, the remainder being fenced off as the school playing fields. A post-war prefabricated community centre stood at the north east corner, once the Headquarters of the 2nd Aldborough Hatch Scout Group and later the Salvation Army. A single storey Mosque now stands on the site. Two further religious groups have premises in Oaks Lane. The Methodist Church, built in 1934, closed early in this century and the buildings were converted in 2008 for the Mata Sahib Kaur Sikh Academy, now a day nursery, whilst the South West Essex and Settlement Reform Synagogue is sited at the rear.

Chase Lane is to the north, leading from Oaks Lane to Horns Road via the bridge over the Central Line (used by those who enjoy walking to Sainsbury's – and there are many, I can assure you, my late wife being one!). Is Chase Lane the 'Lover's-walk' referred to in *The London Gazette*, 13th January 1863, page 195 *(see page 25)*? I like to think it is, for I am a bit of a romantic. The farmland to the north of Chase Lane – the grass of which is now enjoyed by horses grazing there – was excavated for gravel in the late 19th Century, the gravel being used to form the embankment for the railway line from Newbury Park to Barkingside.

Two ladies, one walking her dog and the other on her way to Sainsbury's, in Chase Lane, August 2011. Was this once called "Lover's-walk"? Today the Lane is well-lit with CCTV for safety reasons.

The war-time Wardens' post in July 1943 was in the corner of the field next to 35 Oaks Lane, where the entrance to Oaks Park High School is today. (Back row) Mr Felce, Mr Quinnell, Mr Peacock, Mr Trowbridge, Mr Davis, Mr Naylor, Mr Hulett. (Front Row) Mr Sargent, Mr Gains, Mr Field, Mr Curtis, Mrs Tyson.

Mr Felce lived in one of the houses in the background, Mr Trowbridge and Mr Hulett both lived in Crownfield Avenue, Mr Naylor in Stainforth Road and Mrs Tyson in the last house just behind the hut. David Davis, who sent me this photograph, whose father is in the photograph and who now lives in Somerset, lived at 7 Oaks Lane before moving to St John's Road in January 1944. The son of one of the Wardens was killed by a lorry on the old Newbury Park Station bridge – he was riding his bike at the time.

Hainault Farm

Hainault Farm House (left) and buildings were constructed in 1855 and are Locally Listed. The two-storey Farm House is built with brown stocks with red brick projecting quoins, string course and cornice.

There is a medium-pitch hipped slate roof, double-hung sash windows with glazing bars and/or segmental gauged red brick arches. The south wing has three windows but two ground floor windows have been replaced. The east end of the south wing has a recessed entrance with semi-circular gauged red brick arch, half-glazed door and fanlight. There is a projecting chimney with plaque reading: *'VR 1855'*. The east wing continues with five windows. North west of the Farm House is an enclosed large square farmyard, with two-storey barns on the north and south, and a one-storey barn on the west. They are built from stock brick with medium-pitched gabled slate roofs. The two-storey barns have timber pivot windows with glazing bars. The ground floor is partly open with cast iron columns and timber beams. The one-storey barn has timber louvered ridge vents. The house at the entrance is two-storeys of stock brick, with gabled slate roof and two windows on the first floor. The central entrance has a projecting porch and one window to the ground floor. A terrace of four farmworkers' cottages are of yellow stock bricks with steep-pitch slate roof.

George and Margaret Torrance farmed here and are both buried in St. Peter's Churchyard – Margaret (47) in 1912 and George (81) in 1937. The Poulter family followed. In 1926 John Clark married, bringing his new wife to Hainault Farm, where they set up a dairy business. They had three children, Catherine, Betty and John Mackie – John Mackie was killed in the farmyard by a milk tanker at the age of eight in 1940 and is buried at St. Peter's together with his father, who died in 1949. Alan and Daphne Padfield moved to Hainault Farm in 1959, taking over from Express Dairies. The Milk Marketing Board collected milk from the farm daily until the dairy herd was sold in June 1989, the year that Alan and Daphne moved to Hatfield Broad Oak and their son, Gerald, took over running the farm. Alan was Vicar's Churchwarden at St. Peter's from 1968 to 1978. Sadly, Alan died at the age of 63, but Daphne continues to live at Hatfield Broad Oak.

Fairlop Airfield

There are said to have been three airfields on Fairlop Plain in the First World War (1914-1918) – Hainault Farm Aerodrome (on land to the east of Hainault Road) and Fairlop Aerodrome – both Royal Naval Air Service – and one of the first Royal Flying Corps airfields, which started to operate there from 1915. Twelve service personnel died on active duty from Hainault Farm Aerodrome and the same number from Fairlop Aerodrome. Sopwith Camels, single-seat biplane fighters, were based at the farms and the pilots were involved in shooting down Zeppelins. The 44th Squadron Royal Flying Corps was formed at Hainault Farm on 24th July 1917 as a home defence squadron, gaining fame by pioneering the use of the Sopwith Camel for night operations and achieving the first unqualified victory in combat between aircraft flying at night – two Sopwith Camels versus a German Gotha on the night of 28th/29th January 1918. There is an interesting reference to Fairlop Airfield in the book *Sagittarius Rising* (1936) by Cecil Lewis, who writes: *"I was made a Flight-Commander and posted to No. 44 Squadron stationed at Hainault Farm, just out beyond Ilford in Essex. The squadron was quartered in a large farmhouse by the aerodrome. It was not particularly comfortable; but as Hainault was within three-quarters of an hour of the West End, pilots spent most of their night in town."*

The buildings (left) opposite Hainault Farm are Hangers from the First World War and were almost certainly used in the Second World War (1939-1945) as no permanent Hangers for maintenance were built on Fairlop Airfield. Fairlop Airfield was built in 1939 as an auxiliary airfield to cover Hornchurch, Debden and North Weald in the event of them being unusable through enemy attack. Parts were, sadly, recently demolished.

After the First World War the landing ground reverted to agriculture. During the late 1930s it was purchased by the City of London Corporation with the intention of developing it into a major airport, but the serious world situation brought about by the Munich crisis of 1938 caused the project to be shelved. Fairlop was requisitioned by the Ministry of Defence in September 1940 and became operational 10th September 1941, after the Battle of Britain. The last operational flights took place in March 1944. During the Second World War over 1,000 personnel were stationed on Fairlop Plain. Spitfires and Typhoons were amongst the aircraft which flew from Fairlop. Many service men and women were killed in action and lie buried in Barkingside Cemetery, in the churchyard at Holy Trinity Parish Church, Barkingside, and at St. Mary's Great Ilford. Others killed in action after they flew from Fairlop now lie at peace in various cemeteries in Europe and a few have no known grave. In recent years a Remembrance Day Service has been held on 11th November at Fairlop Waters. After the planes had gone, Fairlop hosted No. 24 Balloon Centre operated mostly by WAAFs with the objective of forming a barrier, with other fields on the East side of London, to bring down V1 rockets (Doodlebugs). Fairlop's balloons were accredited with bringing down 19 V1s out of a total of 278 brought down by balloons. The Station closed in August 1946 and was briefly considered once again as a possible site for a new London Airport (cf. *Essex Airfields in the Second World War,* Graham Smith), but in 1950 the Government decided it should remain an open space and Heathrow was developed as London's airport – a lucky escape for Fairlop.

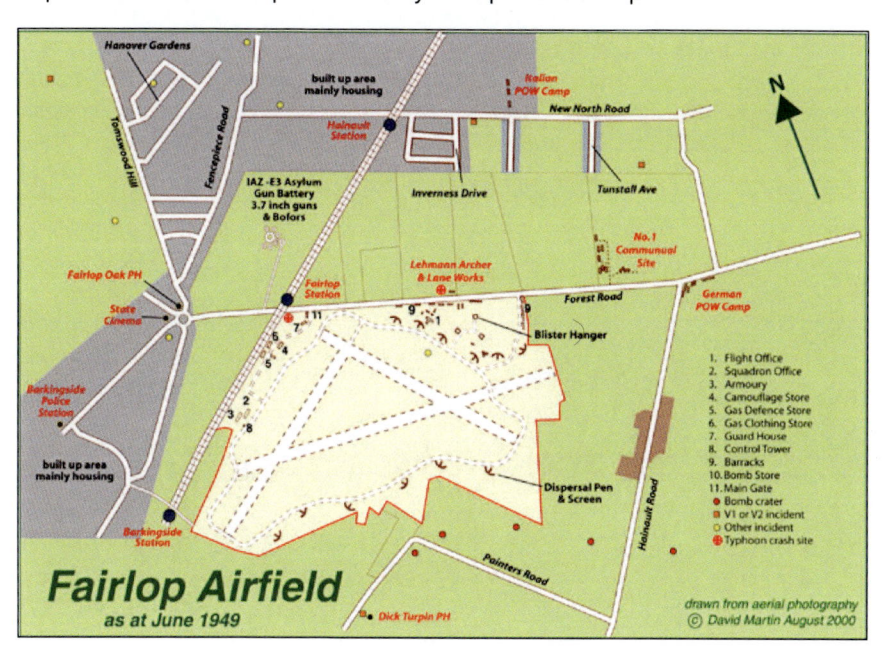

Fairlop Airfield
as at June 1949

drawn from aerial photography
© David Martin August 2000

1. Flight Office
2. Squadron Office
3. Armoury
4. Camouflage Store
5. Gas Defence Store
6. Gas Clothing Store
7. Guard House
8. Control Tower
9. Barracks
10. Bomb Store
11. Main Gate
● Bomb crater
■ V1 or V2 incident
○ Other incident
● Typhoon crash site

I am grateful to David Martin for permission to reproduce the above plan. Two Prisoner of War (POW) Camps are shown – for Germans and Italians (there was a second camp for the latter at Little Heath). Post 1945 motor cyclists roared round on the runways and powered model aircraft flew and zoomed overhead – making walking out on a Sunday afternoon with your girlfriend a hazardous business (especially if you stopped for a kiss and a cuddle!). In the 50s P. T. Read started to extract sand and gravel where the Fairlop Waters golf course stands today, infilling with household rubbish so that when the wind blew plastic bags and such like would descend on Aldborough Hatch to be stuck in trees and hedges. It was not a pretty sight, but more overleaf about sand, gravel and the battles fought on land rather than in the air to preserve our beloved Green Belt of Fairlop Plain.

Fairlop Waters Country Park

Fairlop Waters Country Park is at the northern tip of the parish of St. Peter's Aldborough Hatch. A walk along Bridleway 93, which starts at St. Peter's, takes you past Aldborough House and Aldborough Hatch Farms to a stile entry to Fairlop Waters – although the walker needs to avoid the flying golf balls at this point. A safer, and more relaxed, entrance is to be found at the northern end on Forest Road. Travelling on the Central Line and alighting at Fairlop Station, Fairlop Waters is but a short walk away – using the Zebra Crossing installed in 2010, the walker can be inside the Park within a minute or three or five.

In addition to the flora and fauna of the Country Park, Fairlop Waters has a 38 acre lake for sailing, canoeing and windsurfing. On one of the two large islands a new habitat was created in 2009 to benefit birds such as lapwing, golden and little ringed plover, tern and snipe. Outdoor facilities include 9- and 18-hole golf courses, and a floodlit driving range. For the angler there is a three-and-a-half-acre specimen lake with carp, tench and bream. The sailing lake is available for night fishing, with carp, roach, bream, perch and pike.

Recent renovations at Fairlop Waters include restyling of the seating area outside the function hall/meeting room, bar and restaurant. Here families enjoy the sunshine in July 2011.

But it was not always thus for Fairlop Waters today stands as a monument to what can be achieved when concerned residents and elected Councillors are prepared to stand up to be counted when the openness of the Green Belt is under threat from developers. As seen earlier, Fairlop Plain was part of Hainault Forest until 1851 when the land was farmed for agricultural purposes. In both World Wars parts of the Plain formed Fairlop Airfield. This Crown land was then owned by the London County Council and later by Ilford and Redbridge Councils – the latter two benefiting financially from the highly profitable sand and gravel extraction which took place from the 1950s onwards and continues today. After P. T Read,

Steetleys took over the sand and gravel extraction, followed by Brett Lafarge. At first, infill was domestic rubbish, which left the methane deposits found today in some places, but later inert materials were used. As extraction ended, land was either returned to agricultural use or formed part of today's Fairlop Waters with sailing lake, golf course, fishing lake, Country Park and meeting hall and bar.

In the 1980s the Council granted a developer a 125-year lease (and having been handed a copy of this by a man-in-a-raincoat-on-a-dark-night, I can confirm that any lawyer worth his salt could have driven a coach and horses through it!). In the late 1990s the developer holding the lease applied to Redbridge Council for planning permission to build the London City All-weather Racecourse – and this started a ten-year battle by residents and some Councillors to prevent what they perceived as the desecration of the openness of the Green Belt of Fairlop Plain. Two residents' groups – Barkingside 21 and the Aldborough Hatch Defence Association (AHDA) – were at the forefront of the campaign to keep Fairlop Waters a green open space. The racecourse would have been little more than a dirt track with a huge stand and restaurant facilities and not akin in any way to Ascot or Newmarket, but more like a dog track. Speakers at the Public Inquiry in the summer of 2001 included MPs, Councillors and representatives of the two residents' groups. The arguments for and against are chronicled in the local press and the AHDA *Open Space* newsletters of the time. Suffice to say that public meetings and large numbers attending Council meetings and the Public Inquiry made clear that there was a considerable body of local opinion against the racecourse – and a small minority in favour (some of the latter being folk who thought that their businesses might benefit financially). The Planning Inspector allowed the developer's appeal against the decision by Redbridge Council to reject the planning application, but in the summer of 2002 the Rt. Hon John Prescott, Deputy Prime Minister, overturned the decision. Threats of Judicial Review and a High Court challenge followed, then a revised planning application was submitted – but in 2005 the developer went into administration. Uncertainty on the future of Fairlop Waters was finally resolved in the autumn of 2006 when Redbridge Council bought back the lease from the Administrator for a sum said to be in the region £1,500,000. Announcing the decision, the Leader of the Council said that the site would be *"back in the Council's direct control"* for the racecourse *"was never popular with local people, was opposed by the Council and never seemed in the interests of Redbridge. We have stopped the plan in its tracks and we will improve the site and its facilities for the local community"*. In the years since, Redbridge Council Officers and Councillors, supported by local residents and residents' groups, have worked to fulfil that dream, with financial support from the National Lottery, the Mayor of London and other trusts. New footpaths have been created, tree planting has taken place, new boulder and natural play areas have been installed. Much remains to be done when money becomes available and one day Transport for London may accede to local requests for a bus route from Barkingside – and this finally came to pass in 2016 when the 462 bus was re-routed to Forest Road and a bus stop sited outside Fairlop Waters! Wonders never cease!

The lake at Fairlop Waters in July 2011. Used by schools, youth groups, families and other organisations, the changing facilities are in dire need of refurbishment, but the facility has enabled hundreds of youngsters to enjoy sailing and canoeing.

Deep in the Country Park on a summer afternoon in 2011 – who would guess that we are a mile or so from the busy A12 and a mere dozen miles from Central London? How fortunate we are!

One of the boulders – enjoyed by children for play and by serious rock climbers for practice. The author's grandson peeps over the top!

Aldborough Grange and the Grange Estate

Mrs Verbeke, who contributed to the construction of St. Peter's (see page 23), lived at Aldborough Grange, an 18th Century mansion on the south corner where Applegarth Drive meets Aldborough Road North, opposite the church. The water-colour (left) is by Alfred Bennett Bamford (1857-1939).

I have the deeds of a house in Aldborough Hatch which date back to 1898. These yellowing pages are headed *Abstract of the Title of Stoneley and Co. Ltd. to Freehold Premises formerly part of the Aldborough Grange Estate at Ilford in the County of Essex.* Fascinating they are – but in error in stating that Aldborough Hatch was in the Parish of Barking for by 1898 it was in the parish of St. Peter. There is a list of stipulations: *"No building shall be erected or used as a workshop, warehouse or factory and no noisy, noxious or offensive or manufacturing trade or business shall be carried on nor shall any operative machinery be fixed or placed on any land. No hut, shed, caravan, house on wheels or any other chattel adapted or intended for use as a sleeping or dwelling apartment, nor any booths, swings, roundabouts, contrivances for public amusement or hoarding board (except for building purposes) or station for advertisements shall be erected, made, placed or used or be allowed to remain upon any land nor shall any land be used for the storage of building materials, goods or rubbish and the vendor or the owner or owners of any land to which these stipulations relate may remove and dispose of any such erection or other thing and for that purpose may enter any land upon which a breach of this stipulation shall occur and shall not be responsible for the safe keeping of anything so removed or for the loss thereof or any damage thereto."* I am told by someone who knows that planning controls mean that from 2008/9 you can build virtually any edifice you want and take up 50% of the garden, anything except stables and horses – which means you may have the odd cow, sheep or goat to graze. Sadly parts of the Hatch have become a concrete jungle as a result of this free-for-all planning madness with front and even rear gardens concreted over, and bungalows springing up at the ends of gardens purporting to be used as gymnasia or prayer rooms, complete with showers and kitchens. It's a laugh and few seem to care as once green front gardens become car parks, but I do!

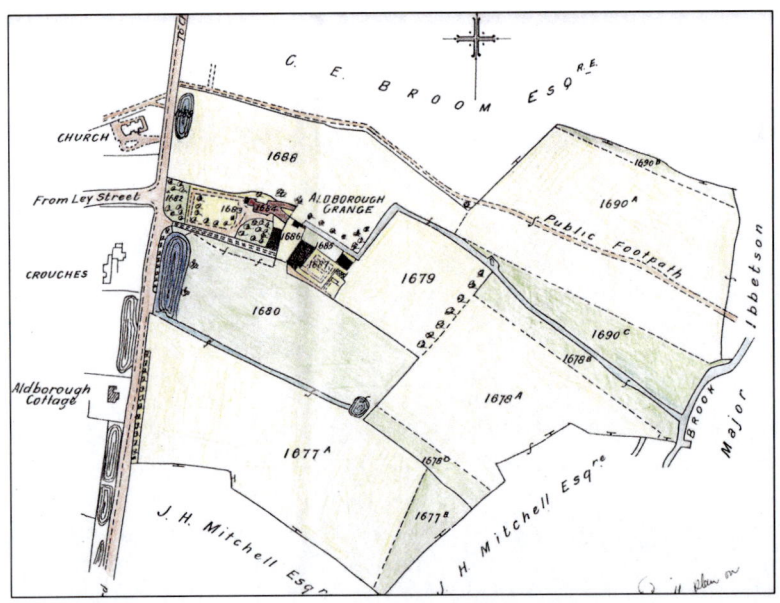

This sketch map forms part of the deeds of some houses built locally in the 1930s and may date before that. The grounds of Aldborough Grange, as seen here, were extensive. The road running from top to bottom on the left is the forerunner of Aldborough Road North. St. Peter's is shown but not the church halls. The road marked 'From Ley Street' is the start of Oaks Lane which led to Ley Street via a footpath and the footbridge over the railway line. The Public Footpath marked from the east side of Aldborough Road North opposite the church runs to what is marked as a 'Brook' – this is Seven Kings Water. Major Ibbetson's land is marked on the east (see pages 16 to 18).

The houses built in the 1930s to the east of Aldborough Road North and north of the A12 were part of the Aldborough Grange Estate. Suburban Developments (London) Limited advertised their 'Type C Improved' houses: *"Come and live here! You'll be happy and house-proud. The Aldborough Grange Estate is 30 minutes from London by London North Eastern Railway (LNER) to Newbury Park Station. Get out at Newbury Park and the Estate is a few minutes' walk along the Ilford to Southend Road* (now the A12). *Open country right at the doors: the seaside less than an hour by coach: Ilford's great shopping centres close by. Everything for everybody!"* Centre houses were priced from £695 (£780 with a brick-built garage). *"£35 deposit and you take possession! There's nothing shoddy about these houses – everything is modern and of the best."* The sketch map shows one of two long ponds on the east side of Aldborough Road North, whilst on the west side three and part of a fourth pond are shown. These ponds explain why the Shrubberies were planted in front of the houses at 42 to 55 Spearpoint Gardens and why the houses from 497 to 511 Aldborough Road North are built back from the road with long front gardens – the houses were built behind the ponds to avoid subsidence. 'Crouches' was a pig and dairy smallholding; the bungalow at 232 Oaks Lane (once signposted 'Little Crouches') is built on this site. 'Aldborough Cottage' is thought to be today's Abury House.

Abury House

Abury House *(left)* was built in 1867 and owned by John Sparks. The grounds covered the land where the house stands today and on which 475, 477, 479, 481, 483, 491 and 493 Aldborough Road North and 2, 4 and 6 Roy Gardens were built in the 1930s. Abury House was sold at the turn of the century to Maria Dormer for £1,600 and in 1929 for £2,200. A caretaker living in Abury House hanged himself in the cellar in 1938 – he was found by John Shope, a local lad who slid down the coal chute to make his find. When the subway at the William Torbitt School opened in 1937, John rode his cycle down the slope, his brakes failed and he crashed into the wall at the bottom and lost all his teeth. The barriers to slow down cyclists were installed as a result – only to be removed in 2011 to allow access for mobility buggies. The two houses north of Abury House were built in 1934 by Amos William Basham – 8 Abury Gardens was sold to Leonard Bird and 10 Abury Gardens to Cecil Frederick Herbert Green. A Memorandum dated February 1947 renamed the houses as 491 and 493 Aldborough Road. Numbers 475, 477, 479, 481 and 483 Aldborough Road North, and 2, 4 and 6 Roy Gardens were built at around the same time. Abury House (the address of which was given in 1867 as Hatch Green in the Parish of Barking) had a large garden and stables – of which the brick wall today in the gardens of 491 and 493 Aldborough Road North is a remnant. A pond in the grounds was later filled in. Abury House was occupied during the Second World War by the Scots Guards (who were also billeted in Spearpoint Gardens) and later as a hostel for nurses, midwives, the mentally unwell and now a hostel for the homeless.

The garden at Abury House in the 1920s.

Newbury Park Station

Newbury Park Station opened on 1st May 1903 as part of the Great Eastern Railway (GER) branch line from Woodford to Ilford via Hainault, known as the Fairlop Loop.

Newbury Park Station and Railway Cottages (left) c1928 when Hatch Lane (now the A12) led to Aldborough Hatch.

Circa 1935 – the shops on the left of the station are Curtis, the Confectioner & Tobacconist (including a tea room), and the office where coal could be ordered from the yard at the side of the station.

Work commenced in 1938 to transfer the line to form the eastern extensions of the Central Line, but this was suspended in 1939 on the outbreak of war, recommencing in 1945. On 29th November 1947 the last steam train ran through Newbury Park and on 14th December 1947 electrified Central Line passenger services commenced from Newbury Park through a tunnel to Leytonstone via Gants Hill and into Central London. In my mind's eye, I can smell the smoke from the engines taking me as a boy from Newbury Park to Ilford – and Bodgers, Wests, Fairheads, Harrison Gibson, Woolworths and the Ilford Hippodrome (to see and enjoy Two-Ton Tessie O'Shea, Old Mother Riley and others).

The Ilford to Newbury Park line in 1936 seen from the road bridge on Vicarage Lane – the railway line to the right ran to Ilford and Liverpool Street Stations, whilst the line to the left carried trains to Seven Kings and beyond into Essex.

The Station with signal box, the station entrance on the bridge and the coal yards on the right. The original entrance building was demolished in 1956 to facilitate the widening of the A12.

The Grade II Listed bus station, designed by Oliver Hill in 1937, erected after the war, opened on 6th July 1949, won a Festival of Britain award (1951). It is high arched with a copper-clad barell-vault roof, 150ft long, 30ft high with seven concrete arches spanning 60ft.

Ilford War Memorial Gardens

The decision to construct a War Memorial in Ilford was taken at a public meeting on 27th November 1918, sixteen days after the Armistice, when the Ilford War Memorial Committee was formed. The following year a 'plebiscite' was taken of all residents in the then Ilford Urban District, with 14,000 votes being cast in favour of a Children's Hospital and a monument. Some £10,000 was donated by those living in the Borough, local businesses and from those with family or other links to Ilford. Two acres near Newbury Park Station were purchased for £800. The Bronze Sentinel mounted on a Cross, erected at a cost of £1,200, was sculpted by Newbury Abbot Trent (1885-1953), a member of the Royal British Society of Sculptors and unveiled by HRH Princess Louise in November 1922. An identical copy of the figure is at Tredegar, Gwent (1924). It took another five years before enough money could be raised to build a new wing to the Ilford Emergency Hospital – The Ilford War Memorial Children's Wing – on land adjoining the Memorial Gardens, part of which was purchased by the Fund. The building included the Memorial Hall *(inset above)* in which the names of the War Dead would be recorded. The total cost was some £8,000. These were opened by Lady Patricia Ramsey, formerly HRH Princess Patricia, the daughter of The Duke of Connaught and a granddaughter of Queen Victoria, on 27th June 1927. The names of the 1,159 men from the Urban District of Greater Ilford, which included Goodmayes, Seven Kings, Newbury Park, Barkingside and Ilford who were killed in the Great War are recorded on panels in the Memorial Hall. The Memorial Hall is a single storey octagonal structure, designed by C. J. Dawson & Allardyce, architects, of red brick with stone dressing, no windows, two doorways, metal and glass ceiling dome. This was to form the main entrance to the Children's Wing, but it was never used for this purpose – perhaps a formidable Matron determined that it would be inappropriate! Apart from use by dignitaries on Remembrance Day in the inter-war years, the Memorial Hall became an adjunct to the Children's Ward, used for storage but on warm days beds were pushed into the Hall and the entrance doors opened to give the children some fresh air.

The Ilford Emergency Hospital became the King George V Hospital, opened by King George V in 1931, and in 1993 that hospital relocated to the grounds of Goodmayes Hospital and is now part of the Barking, Havering and Redbridge University Hospitals NHS Trust. The hospital and maternity hospital nearby were demolished in 2001 to make way for a new housing development. A campaign was mounted to preserve the Memorial Hall and a case was made for the building and the monument at the entrance to the gardens to be added to the statutory list of buildings of special architectural or historic interest (Grade II). Sadly, it was not possible to get the listing extended to the Children's Wing which was demolished. The Memorial Hall (floor area of some 625 square feet) was repaired and refurbished by the developers, Bellway Homes Limited, and ownership transferred to the London Borough of Redbridge. The Hall had fallen into serious disrepair. The panels around the walls and the floor were covered with mould, the masonry was cracked, needing expert repair, and the tiled floor required specialist treatment. It was rededicated in August 2005. In July 2006, the Ilford War Memorial Gardens Action Group – with representatives of local groups, remembrance associations, council officers and chaired by Councillor Ruth Clark – was established to improve the gardens and to increase public awareness of their significance as a place of remembrance and for quiet reflection and relaxation. Improvement works were carried out, daffodils, crocuses and snowdrops planted in the beds and grass, the rose beds restocked and new shrubs planted – with much of the work carried out by members of the Action Group assisted by local residents.

The Gardens were awarded a Certificate of Merit for the most improved public garden by 'London in Bloom' in 2007 and 2008. Information boards now explain the history and significance of the Gardens and Hall. An Open Day in June 2007 commemorated the 80th anniversary of the dedication of the Memorial Hall. A summer concert was held in June 2008 and carol services have been held in the Hall in recent years, decorated with a Christmas tree and holly wreaths. Sadly, the Gardens have experienced their share of vandalism and anti-social behaviour, most notably in 2007 when the glass ceiling lantern was badly damaged by stones thrown from the adjoining footpath. The damage has been repaired. The Gardens are open throughout the day but because of the risk of damage it is not possible to allow unrestricted access to the Memorial Hall. However, a rota of volunteer stewards has been organised, which has enabled the building to be open to the public on Remembrance Sunday and at certain other times during the year.

The Rich and the Famous

Whilst I know a few people in Aldborough Hatch who might be described as rich (but not 'filthy rich' for we would not want any of those, would we?), I doubt if they would wish to feature in these pages and, in any case, I am far too polite to ask questions to establish how rich they are.

However, there are a number of folk who have either lived here or visited who have enjoyed fame of one sort or another. Here, briefly, is what I know about them – but you may know more?

Samuel Pepys: George Tasker records that *"in the days of, and prior to Charles II, numbers of Hainault oaks were cut down for building the King's ships. They were carted to Barking in the first place, and from thence transferred to Woolwich Dockyard and elsewhere. The genial Samuel Pepys, in a note in his diary dated 18th August, 1662, tells of a visit he paid to Hainault, to inspect and check the work of cutting timber for the Royal Navy. He mentions having dined at an inn in Ilford, where he practised how to correctly measure timber."* I like to think that Samuel Pepys journeyed through Aldborough Hatch – if not on his way to the forest, perhaps on the way back, and may even have tarried awhile.

Constance Harvey, eldest daughter of John Donne (1572-1631) lived at Aldborough Hatch with her second husband, Samuel Harvey. Educated at both Oxford and Cambridge, John Donne was a celebrated English poet and preacher and in 1621 King James made him Dean of St. Paul's Cathedral (destroyed in the Great Fire of London in 1666). Oft quoted lines of his are: *"No man is an island, entire of itself; every man is a piece of the Continent, a part of the main".* His poems include such phrases as *"catch a falling star", "for whom the bell tolls",* and *"come live with me and be my love".*
It was at Aldborough Hatch that John Donne, during illness, stayed with his daughter in 1630, the year before his death. Here he revised a sermon preached at The Hague, and here in Aldborough Hatch he made his Will though it was in London that he died in the presence of Izaak Walton *(The Compleat Angler)*, his friend and biographer. Another friend of John Donne was Ben Johnson, English poet and dramatist (1572-1637).

William Stansfield Torbitt was Vicar's Warden at St. Peter's from 1924 to 1932. Born on 15th May 1873, he was Ilford's Director of Education from 1903 to 1938 (that was a long stint in the same job!) and gave his name to the William Torbitt School at the junction of the A12 with Aldborough Road North.
The school was opened on 9th September 1937. I attended shortly after my fifth birthday in March 1938. At some time William Torbitt lived in Stainforth Road, Newbury Park.
He died on 29th January 1945 and is buried with his wife, Kathleen Louise, in Barkingside Cemetery. A new Memorial granite stone was unveiled in 2003 to mark the grave.

Boom Bang-a-Bang in Aldborough Road North!: I first became aware that someone famous lived in the detached house on the opposite side of the road where I live when a white Rolls Royce drove up and out popped Pete Murray, radio and TV presenter, stage and screen actor and disc jockey. Other callers – so I am reliably informed by a lady who knows about these things – included Lulu and Sir Cliff Richard.

Michael Julien lived there with his family and could often be seen sitting at a white grand piano in the lounge at the front of the house.

Michael trained as a teacher at London University, specialising in music and languages. After studying psychology, he obtained an advanced Diploma in Hypnotherapy and then underwent Psychoanalytical training for eight years under a renowned psychiatrist and psychoanalyst. Michael worked as a psychoanalyst and hypnotherapist in Harley Street for more than 20 years, later in an NHS clinic and continued to see clients in his home here in Aldborough Hatch.

I was once hypnotised by Michael at St. Peter's Sunday Club, but that story can wait for another day for it might frighten any children or people of a nervous disposition reading this (and Yvonne preferred not to be reminded of the occasion for we were very young and Michael took me back to my early childhood).

Perhaps it was as a songwriter and composer that Michael will be most popularly remembered. Michael wrote the hit song *Constantly* for Sir Cliff Richard and *Kiss me, honey, honey, kiss* me for Dame Shirley Bassey – the words of which continue, *"Thrill me, honey, honey, thrill me, Don't care even if I blow my top, But, honey, honey, don't stop"*. And all while living in Aldborough Road North, would you believe! He also wrote *Hello Lady* for the Pickwicks.

Michael Julien's greatest claim to fame must be *Boom Bang-a-Bang*, the United Kingdom entry to the Eurovision Song Contest in 1969. It was sung by Lulu and was co-written by Alan Moorhouse and Michael, but under the name Peter Warne, a name he used so as not to confuse his songwriting with his professional life in Harley Street. It was the joint winner with three other entries from Spain, the Netherlands and France.

The song was the second entry with a nonsense title to win and became infamous in the comedy world – most notably inspiring *Monty Python's Flying Circus* to parody it with *Bing Tiddle-Tiddle Bong*. Lyrically, the song is a plea from the singer to her lover to *"cuddle me tight"*. She then goes on to explain that *"my heart goes boom bang-a-bang boom bang-a-bang when you are near"*, complete with appropriate musical accompaniment – which is all somewhat erotic for my taste. The record made UK Number 2 in the singles charts and was a major hit throughout Europe.

Over two decades after its first release, the song was included on a blacklist of banned songs issued by the BBC during the 1991 Gulf War. The title was thought to be too extreme for a war situation. Whilst Lulu was, in fact, singing about how heavy her heart pounds, the BBC thought it sounded a little too much like describing bombs exploding – somewhat far-fetched perhaps! The song is the theme tune to the 2010 BBC3 sitcom *Him & Her*.

Michael retired to live in Hertford and the USA.

It is a fact that Rock Hudson once visited Aldborough Hatch but I will not reveal the details of the house where he stood in the rear garden and was spotted by a former neighbour of mine – for fear that hoards of admirers may stand for days just to soak up the atmosphere of the place. But it came about in this way.

Bryan Forbes – actor, screenwriter, film producer and director, and author – was born John Theobald Clarke on 22 July 1926 in Queen Mary's Hospital, Stratford and grew up in Forest Gate before his parents moved to a mid-terrace house in Spearpoint Gardens, Aldborough Road North (within a stone's throw of my home). Mr Clarke was a commercial traveller, pounding the streets of London selling filing cabinets. In his spare time he was a member of the St John Ambulance Brigade and was often seen in his uniform, trotting off to be of service at a football match or other event. It is a known fact that Mrs. Clarke knitted very fine tea cosies.

Young John Clarke was educated at Godwin Road Elementary and West Ham Secondary Schools, and trained as an actor at the Royal Academy of Dramatic Arts. He was obliged to change his name by British Equity to avoid confusion with the adolescent actor John Clark. After military service from 1945 to 1948, he played numerous supporting roles in British films including in 1955 *The Colditz Story*, alongside John Mills. He also wrote for the screen, receiving his first full credit for *The Cockleshell Heroes* in 1955. A life-long West Ham supporter, his career spanned six decades and he was made a CBE in 2004 for his services to the arts.

Whilst his parents were living in Aldborough Hatch, Bryan Forbes brought film heart-throb Rock Hudson to have tea. Later my neighbour told a good friend of mine that she happened to look out of her rear window when she spotted Rock Hudson in the garden two doors away – and came over all of a quiver! Rock was so impressed with Mrs Clarke's hand-knitted tea cosy that she gave him one which he took back with him to Hollywood. It is also said that Rock and Bryan had a pint up the road at the Dick Turpin. Bryan Forbes and his second wife, Nanette Newman, opened a Vicarage Garden Party at St. Peter's in the late 1950s, offering a signed copy of the script of *The Cockleshell Heroes* for auction – 'Mr T', Reader at St. Peter's, put in the highest bid. I know. I was there at the time.

Lucie Stewart, who lived with her parents, Martyn and Pat, and younger sister Sarah, in Bawdsey Avenue, starred in the West End production of *Annie* in 1978. Then, in 1982, following extensive auditions and trips to the United States, she gained a leading role in the film version of *Annie,* directed by John Huston and choreographed by Arlene Phillips (of *Strictly Come Dancing* fame). Lucie, who played July, one of the orphans, spent six months in Hollywood with her mother – which must have been a terrific experience for a young girl of 9 – and also appeared in the internationally recognised Macy's Day Parade in New York. Lucie subsequently appeared in a variety of theatrical productions and television advertisements before training as a drama teacher. She has since appeared in numerous local theatrical productions, some with Martyn and Sarah, at The Queen's, Hornchurch; Kenneth More, Ilford; and Basildon Towngate Theatres. Now married to Chris, whom she met whilst doing an amateur production of

Grease, they have two sons and live in Essex. Lucie continues to teach drama and also advises on drama and English teaching across the county.

Another actor born in sunny Aldborough Hatch and building a career on TV, in films and on the stage is Sheryl Gannaway. Parents Chris and Margaret are near neighbours of mine, and Sheryl now lives in Epping. Sheryl appeared in the films *Dark Corners* (2006) and *A Girl and a Gun* (2007), and has featured on TV in *Eastenders* as Glynis (2008), *The Bill* as Helen Cooper (2008), *Doctors* as Tilda Locke (2011), *New Tricks* as Caroline Robinson (2011), *Life Begins* and *Dream Team*. Sheryl has toured with the Royal Shakespeare Company and starred nearer home at the Theatre Royal Stratford East, where she played Francis in Martina Cole's *Two Women*, alongside Laura Howard (best known as Cully Barnaby in TV's *Midsomer Murders*) in 2010 and *The Graft* in 2011. Sheryl's friends in Aldborough Hatch will watch her progress with interest in the years ahead.

The Palmerstone School of Dancing has met in St. Peter's Church Halls for many years under the leadership of sisters Loraine Porter and Vicki Palmer *(see page 73)*. Loraine, who first toured in cabaret, appears regularly in shows and pantomimes at Ilford's Kenneth More Theatre, where she is often joined by youngsters from the Palmerstone School. Loraine's son and daughter, Rikki and Tami, are both making their way in show business. Two famous former pupils at the School are Sophie Lawrence and Jenny Powell. Actress Sophie is best known for playing the role of Diane Butcher in the BBC soap opera, *EastEnders*, while presenter Jenny has worked for the BBC and ITV, in ITV's *Wheel of Fortune,* Channel 5's *Wordplay,* BBC's *To Buy or Not to Buy,* and ITV's *Bingo Night Live*.

The 1901 England Census records that George Lansbury lived with his family in The Double House – two adjoining buildings, marked on the 1914 map *(see page 10),* South of Aldborough Hall, on the west side of what is now Aldborough Road North. The buildings were demolished sometime in the early years of the 20th Century, but the cellar area remains within the grounds of the Aldborough Hall Equestrian Centre where it is used today as a cross-country jump. George Lansbury (1859-1940) was a British politician, socialist, Christian pacifist and newspaper editor. Born in Halesworth, Suffolk, he was a campaigner for social justice and improved living and employment conditions for the working class, especially in London's East End. He was a Member of Parliament from 1910 to 1912 and from 1922 to 1940, and leader of the Labour Party from 1932 to 1935.
He lived at the Double House in 1901 with his wife, Elizabeth, and 10 children – the eldest, Bessie (20) was born in Whitechapel and the youngest, Violet (three months) was born in Aldborough Hatch. The Census for 1911 shows the family living in Old Ford, Bow. George and Elizabeth had a total of 12 children. Their granddaughter is the actress Angela Lansbury, perhaps best known for her starring role in the American TV series *Murder, She Wrote* (1984-1996).

Some little-known facts

During my research for this book, I have discovered a number of facts that were unknown to me – and may be unknown to you, too – and some which are known to me and may be known to you, and yet perhaps not . . .

The Queen in Aldborough Hatch: Perhaps the best-known visit of Royalty to Aldborough Hatch (although you may know differently!) was on 25th October 1949 when the then Princess Elizabeth dropped in for tea and cakes at the home of Peter and Wendy Henry at 82 Oaks Lane to mark the $1,000^{th}$ Ilford Council House to be completed since 1945. It is said – and I have it on the best authority – that Mrs Henry became a bit beyond herself about the fact that she had entertained Royalty, but the local ladies put her in her place by reminding her that the furniture had been installed by the Council before the visit and was taken away shortly afterwards in a Harrison Gibson pantechnican!
Also, in 1909 the then Prince and Princess of Wales opened the Fairlop Oak Playing Fields, in 1925 Prince Henry opened the newly built Eastern Avenue, in 1931 King George V and Queen Mary opened King George Hospital, in 1953 The Duke of Edinburgh visited Goodmayes Hospital and in 1989 the Duke of Gloucester visited Fairlop Oak Playing Fields – 80 years after his grandfather's visit.

Murders and rapes: To my knowledge (and, again, you may know differently!), only one murder is recorded on a farm in Aldborough Hatch and that was on Aldborough Hatch Farm in June 2002, when a teacher visiting her parents was tragically killed walking back from Fullwell Cross Swimming Baths. A man was subsequently charged and ordered to be detained indefinitely at a high-security psychiatric hospital. A teenager strangled and knifed his 13-year-old girl friend in Chase Lane in May 1972 and was committed to Broadmoor. I recall a husband murdering his wife in their home in Oaks Lane in more recent years. Rapes were reported to have taken place in Chase Lane at the turn of the century – following which hedges were cut back, lighting improved and CCTV cameras installed to make it the pleasant route to Sainsbury's that it is today.

Suicides: I know of three suicides – a hanging in Abury House in 1938 *(see page 101)*, a shooting in Aldborough House Farm in 1956 *(see page 83)* and a hanging in the butcher's shop in Leyswood Drive in the early 1950s. The butcher at the time was a kindly man called Charlie Churston, who was over-generous in giving customers tick. When they could not pay, Mr Churston watched them walk by on the other side of the road as they went to buy their meat at one of the two butchers' shops on Silverdale Parade. When it all became too much and he was deep in debt, the poor chap hanged himself. Two young brothers, who lived in one of the flats over the shop, were playing in the garden at the rear and spotted his body hanging outside the cold store. All very sad.

Hangings: I have found only one reference to someone associated with Aldborough Hatch being judicially hanged – and I have the late redoubtable Norman Gunby to thank – on 25th May 1785 William Grace was hanged at Chelmsford for stealing a horse in Aldborough Hatch. More than that I know not.

Fairlop Fair and Fairlop Oak: Fairlop Fair was founded early in the 18th Century by Daniel Day (1683-1767), a block- and pump-maker of Wapping, who owned a small estate near Hainault Forest. When he went to receive his rents there, on the first Friday in July, he used to take a party of friends to eat bacon and beans in the shade of the Fairlop Oak. By about 1725 this private picnic had developed into a regular fair. The block- and pump-makers of Wapping used to go there in a large boat mounted on wheels, accompanied by others in wagons, on horseback and on foot. The roistering that accompanied the fair displeased the authorities, who made several attempts to suppress the fair, but it survived Day's death, the destruction of the Oak, and even the disafforestation of Hainault.

About 1856 the government enclosed the site of the fair and shut out the public. The fair was then held successively opposite the 'Old Maypole' at Barkingside, in a field farther along Fencepiece Road, and opposite the 'Bald Hind' at Chigwell. Later it moved back to the 'Old Maypole', where it was still being held in 1900. It appears to have lapsed soon after that.

Fairlop Fair was revived in July 2012 at Fairlop Waters. Traditionally held on the first Friday in July, it has been held successfully on that day every year since. It is a great family event, with many free attractions, different foods on sale, entertainers and great music organised by Chris Wyatt and Steve Collins of the Redbridge Music Lounge. Well worth a visit.

The Fairlop Oak (left), one of the most famous of Essex trees, stood about a mile north-east of Aldborough Hatch, on or near the site of the present Hainault recreation ground, Forest Road. Legend has it that Queen Anne (1666-1714) visited the Oak. A song sheet issued at the Fairlop Fair has a song called "Come, come my boys" in which one of the verses states:

FAIRLOP OAK, 1800

"To Hainault Forest Queen Anne did ride,
And saw the old oak standing by her side,
And as she looked at it from bottom to top,
She said to her Court, it should be at Fairlop."

Peter Kalm, the Swedish naturalist, who visited the Oak in 1748, measured the circumference of the trunk, at a height of 4 ft. from the ground, as 30 ft. and the spread of the branches as 116 ft. By the end of the 18th Century the tree was moribund; a writer of 1791 thought that its decay had been hastened by the lighting of fires in the bole during the fairs. After further damage by fire in 1805 the oak was blown down in 1820. Part of it is said to have been made into a pulpit and reading-desk for the new church of St. Pancras, Woburn Place, London. The remains of the tree were uprooted with the rest of Hainault Forest in 1851. In 1909 a new oak was planted in the recreation ground, on a site thought to be that of the old one. Another tree, called the 'new Fairlop Oak' was planted on the green at Fullwell Cross in 1951.

This old footpath (left) across Seven Kings Water (also known as Seven Kings Brook) in more rural days is the one from the Bury and Great Newburys Farm to Little Heath or the one southward from Aldborough Hatch. Seven Kings Water has its source in the lake at Hainault Forest, runs under the A12 at what I called Happy Valley in my youth, skirting Barley Lane and Seven Kings Park and onwards to South Park and Barking. Had I been asked the derivation of Barley Lane I would have guessed that it has something to do with fields of barley, but I could not have been more wrong! Before the Dissolution, the Abbess of Barking was Dorothy Barley, who gave her name to the road that runs from Little Heath to the Romford Road and is clearly marked on Cary's survey of 15 miles around London dated 1786 (see page 5).

Bennett and Williams at Plessey's Sports Ground: A highlight of the summer months in Aldborough Hatch in the immediate post-war years was the annual sports day at the Plessey's Sports Ground (later the Barley Mow), on the land in Oaks Lane on which Oaks Park High School stands today. I remember little of what happened during the daytime for it was the evening's variety show that attracted me with top-of-the-bill Music Hall acts including Bennett and Williams, whose cross-talk banter was fast and furious, ending with them playing strange instruments like a cello, but instead of an acoustic body, the sound came out of a brass horn attached to the end – I believe it was called a violano virtuoso or a one-string fiddle. Deep, deep in the memories of my youth, I recall seeing Morecombe and Wise at the same venue, but I think that is very unlikely and a figment of my imagination (although you may know differently, of course).

According to the National Bell Register, the single bell in the Belfry at St. Peter's was cast in 1861 by George Mears at Whitechapel Bell Foundry, which dates back to at least 1570, but a continuous line of master founders in Whitechapel or nearby Aldgate exists since 1420. The Vicar reported at the

Parochial Meeting on 23rd April 1927 that the *"the bell had been re-hung, new lightening conductor and weathercock provided."*

(Above) Lake Cottages, built in 1871 (a plaque on the west wall records this) between Aldborough House Farm and Aldborough Hatch Farm, opposite the Chapel. The west wall was blown down in the gales on 15th/16th October 1987 – at the same time as the Chapel was damaged (see page 14). The rear garden wall (inset) is Locally Listed and is said to date to Tudor times; there may be remains hereabouts from the Mesolithic to the Romano-British periods.

A relic of the Second World War, these concrete blocks at the West end of Chase Lane (left) were built to deter the enemy as tank traps in parks, farmland and open spaces where a tank might be driven – and were known as Dragon's teeth. When taking this photograph I asked an adult passing by why the blocks were put there – for young people to sit on, he said!

Listed Buildings in Aldborough Hatch

A Listed Building, placed on the **Statutory List of Buildings of Special Architectural or Historic Interest,** may not be demolished, extended or altered without special permission from the local planning authority.
There are three types of listed status for buildings in England and Wales:
Grade I: buildings of exceptional interest.
Grade II*: particularly important buildings of more than special interest.
Grade II: buildings of special interest, warranting every effort to preserve them.

Locally Listed Buildings – some buildings not of national importance, but of local architectural or historic interest, make a contribution to the character of the Borough. Redbridge Council maintains a List of these buildings and seeks to preserve them. The Council values these buildings in all their diversity and wishes to see them maintained. The Council has no additional legal powers to protect Locally Listed Buildings but has adopted a policy (E3) for their preservation within its Local Development Framework. If a planning application is made for a Locally Listed Building the Council will take account of the impact of the proposals upon the special architectural or historic interest for which the building was locally listed.

Statutory Listed Buildings in the Parish of Aldborough Hatch – Grade II *(The Memorial Gardens are strictly outside Aldborough Hatch, but I include them nonetheless – and why not!)*
St. Peter's Church, Aldborough Road North – 1862
Former Chapel attached to Aldborough Hall, Oaks Lane – 1730
Newbury Park Station Bus Shelter – 1937
War Memorial, Eastern Avenue – 1922
War Memorial Hall, Eastern Avenue – 1927
Locally Listed Buildings in the Parish of Aldborough Hatch
Farm Workers' Cottages, 1-4 Hainault Works, Hainault Road (east side) – 1855
Farm workers' Cottages, Hainault Farm, Hainault Road (west side) – 1855
Hainault Farm, Farmhouse, Hainault Road – 1855.
Farm buildings, Hainault Farm, Hainault Road – 1855
House at entrance to Hainault Farm, Hainault Road – 1855
Garden walling and former Gazebo, south of the Dick Turpin Inn, Aldborough Road North – 18th Century.
Former school adjacent to St. Peter's Church, Aldborough Road North – 1867
Former Garden Wall, r/o 211-233 Oaks Lane – circa 1800 *(or earlier)***
Aldborough Hatch Farm Barn, Oaks Lane – circa 18th Century
Barn B, Aldborough Hatch Farm, Oaks Lane – circa 1850
Garden walls r/o 1-2 Lake Cottages, Oaks Lane – 18th Century *(or earlier)***
Whites Farm, Farmhouse, Oaks Lane – Circa 1860
Hainault House, No 9, Little Heath, Chadwell Heath – late 18th Century
Goodmayes Hospital, Barley Lane (and Peripheral Buildings) – circa 1901

*** *My italics – possibly earlier than stated in Local Listing by Redbridge Council*

March 2017

Sand, Gravel and the Aldborough Hatch Defence Association

On pages 96 and 97 I refer briefly to the extraction of sand and gravel on Fairlop Plain by a series of developers – now Brett Tarmac Limited. This is intrinsically linked to the formation of the Aldborough Hatch Defence Association.

Some sand and gravel extraction had been carried out on Fairlop Plain in the late 19th and early 20th Centuries, but major extraction commenced in the 1950s where the golf course is today. When the wind blew Aldborough Hatch was attractively covered in paper and plastic from the household refuse infill until the contractors were instructed to cover with soil every evening.

Initially there was little interest in Aldborough Hatch, but in the mid-1960s a planning application was submitted to extract on Aldborough Hatch Farm over the area stretching north from St. Peter's up to the present southern boundary of Fairlop Waters. The Revd Bill Barnes, Vicar of St. Peter's, formed the Aldborough Hatch Defence Association (AHDA) shortly after his induction in 1966 to monitor and protect the environment of Aldborough Hatch and specifically to ensure that the proposed sand and gravel extraction did not have a disastrous effect on the buildings of St. Peter's and Aldborough Hatch Chapel. Founder members of the AHDA included Joan Sullivan, Ron King, John Coombes and John Debere. Early members included Vivien Bendall and Linda Perham, then MPs for Ilford North, Frank Sinclair, Kip Pedge and Chris Gannaway.

The Revd Barnes led the campaign for a buffer zone of 300 yards from the Church and spoke forcefully at the Ilford Council Planning Committee. When Councillors appeared to be prepared to agree to the excavations running up to Bridleway 93 and the northern hedge of the churchyard, there was pandemonium in the public gallery. I sat between the Revd Barnes and Vivien Bendall MP – and we three led the booing! It was great fun I recall – until the Mayor, Councillor (later Alderman) Dalton, had all three of us ejected physically (we had to be carried out!). He closed the meeting and allowed us back, but warned that should we continue with this very naughty behaviour, the consequences would be more than dire (in fact, we feared we might be buried under the excavations!). But the battle for a 300-yard buffer was won! When planning applications were submitted for later excavations – at Hainault Farm and Aldborough Hall Farm – the AHDA pressed for stand-off buffer zones of 300 yards – but we were successful in gaining 150 metres from houses in Billet Road and Applegarth Drive/Bawdsey Avenue. Excavation at Aldborough Hall Farm went ahead – taking over 14 years rather than the promised six. Work continues to restore the land for nature conservation with the AHDA taking a keen interest in making sure that the work is to a high standard and accessible to the public to enjoy.

In 2006 we were advised that Lafarge would be submitting a planning application to excavate on Aldborough Hatch Farm over the area bordering Aldborough Road

North, St. Peter's Church, St. Peter's Close and Oaks Lane. But it was not until ten years later (after Brett Tarmac staged two exhibitions at which residents made their objections crystal clear) in May 2016 that planning application 2089/16 was posted for extraction on land at both Aldborough Hatch and Hainault Farms. In the first eight months over 160 objections were registered by residents and interested organisations. The AHDA is in the forefront of the Enough is Enough Campaign to end sand and gravel extraction in the area. As we go to press we await news of the planning application being considered by Redbridge Council's Regulatory Committee when the AHDA will put its views forcefully. For details of our numerous and serious objections please see the AHDA website at www.theahda.org.uk.

At last – Lifts at Newbury Park Station!

Yes, that was promised by Sadiq Khan, Mayor of London, when he visited the station in December 2016. In 2009 Transport for London (TfL) spent £4.5M on new lifts, then ran out of money, so dished out a further £1.4M filling in the shafts! Now the lifts are going to be unveiled in 2017. We are keeping our fingers crossed.

Community Garden for Aldborough Hatch

A small group of volunteers from St. Peter's Church and the local area, led by Abi and Kristy Leach, worked throughout 2016 on creating a new garden at the far end of the churchyard. This involved erecting new fencing, cutting out a bark-covered footpath with arches at each end, and planting and cultivating sensory shrubs, a wildflower bank and spring bulbs, with fresh vegetables in raised beds. A very welcome grant of £10,000 from Tesco's Bags of Help Scheme will enable more work to be carried out around the Memorial Wall with fresh planting throughout 2017 and a gate being installed, leading from the Vicarage to the churchyard, as in the distant past.

*(Left) Members of the team work to make a pathway in the new garden at St. Peter's Church
(from left to right) Vanessa Cole, Kristy Leach, Ashley Briscoe, Chris Gannaway and Abi Leach.*

(Right) The wildflower bank in summer 2016, looking over the hedge to Fairlop Plain and Fairlop Waters Country Park.

Dick Turpin and Cuckoo Hall Orchards

Further to pages 76 to 80, the Aldborough Hatch Defence Association (led by Jenny Chalmers) worked with The Orchard Project (with Stephanie Irvine, Orchard Restoration Project Manager) started work in the summer of 2016 to restore the orchard trees in the rear car park at the Dick Turpin and Cuckoo Hall – with days working to clear brambles and ivy shading the 100-year-old fruit trees, and a pruning day with veteran tree expert Russell Miller. The 1st Aldborough Hatch Guides, led by Louise Wilson, and students from the William Torbitt Primary School took an active part as they learned from experts in orchard husbandry how to protect and enhance the environment to ensure that the orchard continues to provide fruit for the local community.

Before work could commence on restoring the orchard trees at Cuckoo Hall, many years' growth of brambles and ivy had to be cleared. Some members of the team get stuck in (from left to right) Abi Leach, Chris Gannaway, Ken Morgan and Kristy Leach.

Pruning the pear tree in the Dick Turpin orchard in January 2017 (from left to right) Suzanne Batey, Chris Gannaway, Russell Miller, Stephanie Irvine and Jenny Chalmers.

A final thought

As the sub-title off this book indicates, Aldborough Hatch is considered by some (me amongst them) to be akin to a village. The A12 to the south acts as a river (only to be crossed in safety at certain defined points, for the vehicles travel along that arterial road at speeds that are best forgotten), with the Central Line to the west (not to be crossed except by the bridge running from Chase Lane to Sainsbury's or that at Newbury Park Station), Fairlop Waters to the north (the 'jewel in the crown of Redbridge' as one renown Councillor once described it) and the windy openness of Fairlop Pain to the east (and, my, the wind it doth blow across those fields mightily at times, to be sure).

Many of us like it that way and spend time endeavouring to ensure that the Hatch (as it is known with affection) is a pleasant place in which to live, to work and play. Long may it continue and if in our keenness to keep it that way we ruffle a few feathers amongst the hierarchy, so be it. We apologise (for we were brought up to be polite), but we do so simply because we value and enjoy this place on the edge of London's precious green belt (which countless politicians have gone on record as saying is 'sacrosanct'). And I like to think the hierarchy understand - or most of 'em, anyway!